Hawaii for Free

Hundreds of Free Things
to Do in Hawaii

Frances Carter

Maps by Z. Harris

Mustang Publishing
New Haven

*To David,
my friend and partner on the Path*

Distributed to the trade by Kampmann & Company, 9 East 40th Street, New York, NY, 10036.

Library of Congress Cataloging in Publication Data:

Carter, Frances.
    Hawaii for free.

    1. Hawaii--Description and travel--
1981-   --Guide-books. I. Title.
DU622.C37   1988   919.69'044   88-60468
ISBN 0-914457-21-7 (pbk.)

10 9 8 7 6 5 4 3 2

Message from
Gov. John Waihee

Hawaii is a wonderful place to enjoy.

We who live here know that many of the best attractions and activities in the Islands are provided by State and County. What some people may not realize is just how many of these attractions there are. *Hawaii for Free* is the first comprehensive guide of this nature, and it offers something for everyone.

State parks, campgrounds, tennis courts, swimming pools, concerts, botanical gardens and historical sites are just part of the fun things to enjoy in Hawaii which are provided and maintained by local government. They are part of our people's way of life and of Hawaii's unique tradition.

This guidebook offers a new perspective on part of what makes up the magic that is Hawaii. We invite you to partake of Hawaii's abundance, share in our aloha spirit and learn to love our land the way we do.

John Waihee

KAUAI

Lihue

NIIHAU

OAHU

Honolulu

MOLOKAI   Kalaupapa

Wailuku

LANAI   MAUI

KAHOOLAWE

HAWAII

Hilo

The Hawaiian Islands

Map not drawn to scale.

Contents

Introduction

Hawaii is famous for its pristine beaches and awesome scenic attractions, but few visitors know that there are hundreds of great things to do and see in the Islands that are absolutely **free**.

This guidebook will tell you where to find ancient archaeological sites, sample Maui wine and Maui Lager beer, stargaze atop Mauna Kea, visit the country's only rainforest zoo, take guided hikes through gorgeous botanical gardens, attend films at an international film festival, watch Japanese folk dancing, and much more. And nothing costs one penny!

The material is organized by Island: Oahu, Maui, Hawaii, Kauai, Molokai, and even Lanai. Activities are grouped in categories to make it easier to find your favorites, even if you don't know the specific name of a place. And to give you a general idea of where things are located, the number beside each item corresponds to the number on the Island's map.

Since you should verify times and admissions policies before going to any of these attractions, we have tried to provide a telephone number for each entry whenever possible. Please understand that times, dates, and prices may have changed since this guide went to press.

We welcome your comments and suggestions for future editions of *Hawaii for Free*. Please write to me in care of Mustang Publishing, P. O. Box 9327, New Haven, CT 06533. Enjoy!

Frances Carter

Island of Oahu

*T*he Island of Oahu, the third largest of the Hawaiian islands, is the major center of Hawaii's activity. Home to most of the state's residents, Oahu also hosts over five million visitors each year.

Oahu is an island of contrasts and diversity. A drive around the island will take you from the densely packed hotels and condominiums of Waikiki, through fields of pineapple and sugar cane, to world-famous surfing beaches. A walk through downtown will take you past some of Hawaii's most historic buildings, including the only royal palace on American soil. A glance around at the downtown workers will reveal the ethnic mixture prevalent in the islands: Japanese, Caucasian, Chinese, Filipino, Korean, Hawaiian, and Vietnamese.

Most of Hawaii's visitors spend at least part of their stay in Waikiki, the playground of the Pacific. This short stretch of land in the shadow of Diamond Head is packed with an array of shops selling everything from plastic hula dolls to $5,000 handbags. If visitors tire of shopping, they can enjoy surfing, sailing, canoeing, a visit to a zoo, an aquarium, a museum, numerous festivals, and food galore.

At one end of Waikiki is the Honolulu Zoo, home to over 2,000 creatures and a popular (and free) evening concert in the summer. At the other end is Fort DeRussy Museum, with an impressive display of military memorabilia.

An exploration of Waikiki is not complete without a hike to the summit of Diamond Head. The trek begins inside the crater at Diamond Head State Park and continues up a well-maintained trail through a catacomb of dark hallways, tunnels, and a climb up 99 concrete steps.

Diamond Head got its nickname back in the 1800's when British sailors found calcite crystals—which looked like diamonds. To the early Hawaiians, Diamond Head was sacred. Of the five *heiaus* (temples) that were once on the mountain, the remains of only one exist today.

In 1904, the U.S. government bought Diamond Head and 700 acres around the crater for $3,300. During World War II, hundreds of soldiers occupied barracks in the crater, but their guns were never used. In 1950, the Army removed its equipment, and Diamond Head was designated a national monument in 1968.

Art

1. **Art Mart**—*along the fence of the Honolulu Zoo on Monsarrat Ave.* This outdoor display of works of local artists is held every Wednesday, Saturday, and Sunday from 10:00am to 4:00pm.

2. **Contemporary Museum**—*605 Kapiolani Blvd., inside the News Building.* The works of Oahu's leading artists are exhibited here in shows which usually last about six weeks. Open Monday through Friday 8:30am to 5:00pm, and Saturday from 8:30am to 1:00pm. Phone: 526-1322.

3. **Honolulu Academy of Arts**—*900 South Beretania St.* Honolulu's most important art center, the Honolulu Academy of Arts is best known for its collection of oriental art, but it also has a fine collection of European, American, and contemporary Hawaiian art. The beautiful building, with six courtyards and 37 gallery rooms, is itself a work of art. Mrs. Charles M. Cooke donated money, her oriental art collection, and her homesite to help start the Academy in 1927.

   The Academy also has a theater, an education center,

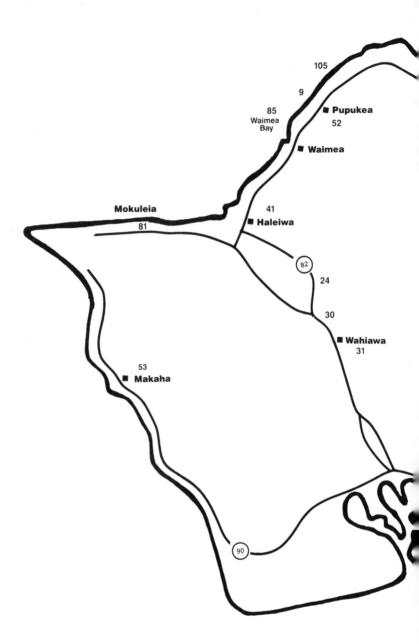

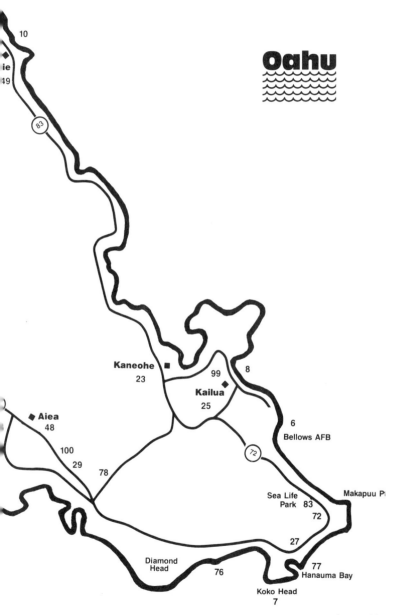

Oahu

10

ie
49

83

Kaneohe ■
23

99   8

Kailua ◆
25

■ Aiea
48

100

29   78

6
Bellows AFB

72

Sea Life   83
Park

72

Makapuu P

27

Diamond
Head   76

77
Hanauma Bay

Koko Head
7

and the Garden Cafe. Open 10:00am to 4:30pm Tuesday through Saturday, and 1:00pm to 5:00pm on Sunday. Free guided tours are offered Tuesday through Sunday. Call 538-1006 for times of tours and current activities.

4. **Tennent Art Foundation Gallery**—203 *Prospect St.* This gallery is devoted to displaying the works of the late Madge Tennent, who specialized in large Polynesian figures. Open Tuesday through Saturday 10:00am to noon, and Sunday 2:00pm to 4:00pm. Phone: 531-1987.

Beach Parks

5. **Ala Moana Beach Park**—*Ala Moana Blvd., across from Ala Moana Shopping Center.* The favorite beach of many Honolulu residents, Ala Moana has picnic facilities, a jogging trail, tennis courts, snack bars, an outdoor gym, and a calm swimming area. On Fridays around 5:30pm it's fun to watch the sailboats put up their colorful spinnakers and sail out of the Ala Wai Yacht Harbor for their weekly races. This is also a good spot to watch outrigger canoe paddlers practice after work.

6. **Bellows Field Beach Park**—*Kalanianaole Highway, just after Waimanalo.* This beach park is owned by the military and is open to the public only on weekends, so it is still a secret gem. Beautiful sandy beaches, calm swimming conditions, and plenty of picnic facilities make this spot a wonderful weekend retreat. Open to the public from noon Friday to midnight Sunday, and dawn to midnight on holidays.

7. **Hanauma Bay**—*7455 Kalanianaole Highway, at the foot of Koko Head.* Hanauma Bay is a unique crater bay and the most popular destination for snorkelers and scuba divers on Oahu. The bay has been a marine reserve since 1967 and has over 90 species of fish—many of which will eat from your hand. Hanauma Bay is so picture perfect, it has been

Hanauma Bay, the most popular snorkeling spot on Oahu.

the setting in several movies, including *From Here to Eternity* and *Blue Hawaii*.

8. **Kailua Beach Park**—450 Kawailoa Rd., eastern end of Kailua Bay in Kailua. There's a 30-acre park with a wide sandy beach, picnic facilities, and safe swimming here. This is also one of the most popular spots for windsurfing.

9. **Pupukea Beach Park**—59-727 Kamehameha Highway. This is one of the best snorkeling and diving spots on the North Shore during the summer. Shark's Cove at the Kahuku end of the beach park has lovely tidal pools and a beautiful cove. Don't be scared off by the name; it's not really a hangout for sharks. And don't attempt to swim here in the winter because the surf is too treacherous.

Camping

There are numerous free campsites on Oahu, but you must obtain a permit from the Division of State Parks, 1151 Punchbowl St., Room 310, which also has a map and list of sites. Call 548-7455 for more information. Some camp sites are safer than others, so it's probably best to talk to people who know the area first. One personal favorite is

10. **Malaekahana State Recreation Area**—*two miles past Laie on Highway 83*. Situated along the beach of Malaekahana Bay, this lovely park is one of the nicest and safest camping sites on the island, and it's usually not crowded. Be sure to pick up a permit first.

Craft Fairs

There are numerous craft fairs around the island throughout the year. They are usually listed in the activities column of the daily newspapers.

11. **Pacific Handcrafters Guild Craft Fairs**—*Ala Moana Park and Thomas Square, across from the Honolulu Academy of Art.* This group schedules four craft fairs each year. They are held the first weekend in May at Ala Moana Park; the third weekend in July at Thomas Square; the first weekend in October at Ala Moana Park; and the first weekend in December at Ala Moana Park. Call 538-1600 for more information about the Guild.

Entertainment

12. **Amateur Night**—*Croissanterie, 222 Merchant St.* Amateur musicians and singers have an opportunity to perform before an audience at this sidewalk cafe. Every Friday from 7:00pm to 11:00pm. Phone: 533-3443.

13. **Downtown Block Party**—*Merchant St., between Nuuanu and Bethel*. Takes place Friday evenings from 6:30pm to midnight, and features a live band, street dancing, and vendors. Sponsored by the Downtown Merchants Association.

14. **King's Village**—*131 Kaiulani Ave., opposite the Hyatt Regency Waikiki*. King's Village is a cute complex of cobblestoned walkways, boutiques, and restaurants with a turn-of-the-century theme. The King's Guards, dressed in monarchy-period uniforms, perform a "Changing of the Guard" ceremony at 6:15pm daily. Look also for Monarch's Walk, with a history of Hawaii's kings and queens, and the Variety Club Celebrity Circle, with permanent hand imprints of famous personalities.

15. **Kodak Hula Show**—*Monsarrat Ave. in Kapiolani Park*. The Kodak Hula Show has been staged since 1937 and is the longest-running show in Hawaii. Women of the Royal Hawaiian Girls Glee Club sing, strum guitars, and dance in muumuus and grass skirts. From January through August, the show is performed at 10:00am Tuesday through Friday. From September through December, shows are Tuesday through Thursday at 10:00am. It's recommended that you arrive at least 45 minutes before showtime to get a seat. Phone: 833-1661.

16. **Mayor's Aloha Friday Lunch Break Concert**—*Tamarind Park, corner of Bishop and King*. Every Friday at noon, performers provide entertainment to downtown workers and visitors. Several eateries around the park are good places to grab a plate lunch and have an impromptu picnic during the concerts.

17. **Polynesian Cultural Center Mini Show**—*Royal Hawaiian Shopping Center, fountain courtyard, 1st floor, Building C*. Polynesian songs and dances are performed by the Polynesian Cultural Center performers every Tuesday, Thursday, and Saturday at 9:30am.

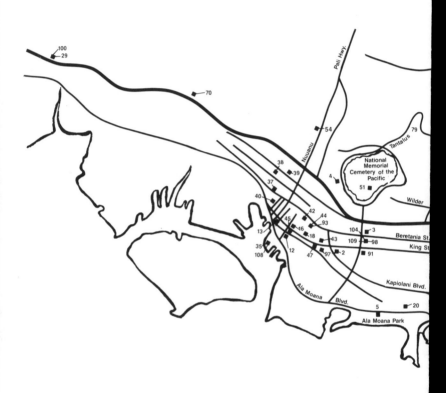

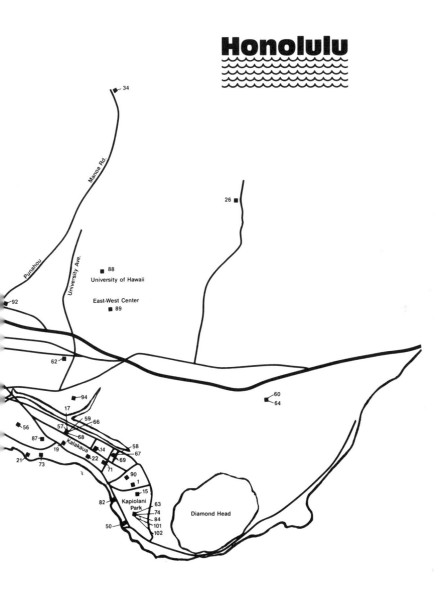

Honolulu

34

26

88
University of Hawaii

East-West Center
89

92

62

94

60
64

17

56
59 66
57
87
68
Kalakaua
19
14
58
67
22
69
21
73
71
90
7

15

82
Kapiolani
Park
63
74
84
101
102

50

Diamond Head

18. **Royal Hawaiian Band**—*Iolani Palace Bandstand, corner of King and Richards.* The band performs Hawaiian, popular, and light classical music every Friday at 12:15pm on the grounds of the Iolani Palace, a great place to have a picnic lunch. The band also performs at the Kapiolani Park Bandstand on Sundays at 2:00pm. Phone: 523-5331.

19. **Waikiki Calls**—*Waikiki Shopping Plaza, 4th floor showroom.* In this audio/visual salute to the Pacific, dancers present scenes from Waikiki's past and present in two 45-minute shows nightly (except Sunday), at 6:15pm and 7:45pm.

20. **Young People's Hula**—*Ala Moana Shopping Center stage.* This lively Polynesian revue features songs and dances of Hawaii, Tahiti, Samoa, and New Zealand performed by students of Kapiolani Butterworth, every Sunday at 9:30am.

Exercise

21. **Exercise Class**—*On the lawn at Fort DeRussy Beach, Waikiki.* For 18 years, this exercise class has been meeting at 9:00am, Monday through Saturday. All ages are welcome; just bring a towel or mat. Phone: 949-8347.

    There is also an exercise class which meets at 8:45am Monday, Wednesday, and Friday, on the lawn fronting the Honolulu Zoo.

Fashion Show

22. **Hyatt Regency Waikiki**—*2424 Kalakaua, in the open courtyard of the Great Hall.* Every Wednesday at 4:00pm, models display the latest fashions as they parade through the courtyard of the Hyatt. Phone: 922-9292.

Gardens

23. **Haiku Gardens**—46-316 Haiku Road, Kaneohe. The lovely gardens here were formerly the grounds of a private estate which has been converted into a restaurant. The gardens are frequently used as a setting for weddings and photo sessions. Open Tuesday through Sunday. Phone: 247-6671.

24. **Helemano Plantation**—64-1510 Kamehameha Highway in Wahiawa, next to the Dole Pineapple Pavilion. This five-acre complex is planted with a variety of flowers, fruits, vegetables, and trees and is maintained by people with disabilities as part of a vocational training program. There's also a restaurant, gift shop, and catering service on the premises, plus lei-making classes, hula lessons, and tours of the complex. For more information, call 622-3929.

25. **Ho'omaluhia Botanic Garden Guided Nature Walk**—end of Luluku Rd. in Kaneohe. This 400-acre botanic garden and nature conservancy on the windward side of Oahu is planted with trees and shrubs from different regions of the world. There is also a 32-acre lake, hiking and riding trails, an exhibition hall, and classrooms.

    The guided nature walks are Saturdays (3.4 miles) at 10:00am and Sundays (2 miles) at 12:30pm. Bring light raingear, insect repellent, walking shoes, and lunch. Call 235-6636 for reservations and for information about special events.

26. **Kawamoto Orchid Nursery**—2630 Waiomao Homestead Rd., Palolo. This commercial orchid nursery lets you browse through rows and rows of numerous orchid species which they pack and ship all over the world. Open Monday through Saturday 7:30am to 4:00pm. Phone 732-5808.

27. **Koko Crater Botanical Gardens**—inside Koko Crater, off Kealahou St. Though the garden doesn't have a wide variety of flora, it offers a nice hiking trail which makes a loop

through the crater and passes a collection of cacti and succulents. There is also a plumeria grove with numerous species of plumeria trees. Phone: 533-3406.

28. **Lyon Arboretum**—3860 M*anoa* R*d*. An affiliate of the University of Hawaii, this arboretum has over 200 acres of botanical gardens with ginger, bromeliads, heliconia, and numerous flowering trees. Tours are offered on the first Friday and third Wednesday of the month at 1:00pm, and the third Saturday at 10:00am. Phone: 988-3177.

29. **Moanalua Gardens**—2850A M*oanalua* R*d*. This private park is open to the public and contains ancient monkeypod trees and a cottage built over 100 years ago for Kamehameha V. This is also the site of the Prince Lot Hula Festival held the third Saturday of July. Open from 7:00am to 6:00pm. Phone: 833-1944.

30. **Pineapple Variety Garden**—K*amehameha* H*ighway and* K*amanaui* R*d., a mile past the* D*ole* P*ineapple* P*avilion*. About 30 varieties of pineapple are displayed in this garden, which illustrates the evolution of the plant that originated in Brazil and has become a staple in Hawaii's economy. Phone: 621-8408.

31. **Wahiawa Botanical Gardens**—1396 C*alifornia* A*ve*. A lovely oasis in Wahiawa containing 27 acres of exotic trees from around the world, the Wahiawa Botanical Gardens is open from 9:00am to 4:00pm. Phone: 621-7321.

Garment Factory

32. **Hilo Hattie's Factory, Kodak Hula Show, and Dole Pineapple Cannery Tour.** From Waikiki and Ala Moana Shopping Center, Hilo Hattie's has shuttle buses which take visitors to the Dole Pineapple Cannery for a film tour of the cannery and samples of pineapple juice, then on to

Hilo Hattie's Fashion Center for a tour of the garment factory where workers create muumuus, aloha shirts, and swimwear. Also at the center is a macadamia nut factory, where visitors can watch nuts being processed into candies and snacks. On the days of the Kodak Hula Show, the tour includes the show. The shuttle buses run every 20-30 minutes and stop at most major hotels in Waikiki. Visitors are returned to Waikiki after the tour. Call 537-2926 for pickup times and locations.

Hiking

Hikers can obtain sectional maps of Oahu trails by writing the State Department of Land and Natural Resources, Division of Forestry and Wildlife, 1151 Punchbowl St., Honolulu, HI 96813, or by calling (808) 548-8850. They don't have an overall map of Oahu, but they will give maps of different sections of the island. Craig Chisholm's book *Hawaiian Hiking Trails* (The Touchstone Press, PO Box 81, Beaverton, OR 97005) or Robert Smith's *Hiking Oahu* (Wilderness Press, 2440 Bancroft Way, Berkeley, CA 94704) contain descriptions of many of the over 80 hiking trails on Oahu.

If you are in good shape, absolutely do not miss the climb up Diamond Head:

33. **Diamond Head**—*Enter about one block east of Diamond Head Road and Makapuu Avenue, which takes you through a tunnel into the crater.* A short (0.7 mile), easy-to-follow trail goes up to the 760-foot peak of Diamond Head to the remains of a gun emplacement from World War II. There are over 100 steps, so this hike isn't for people with heart problems. Another easy, popular hike which takes you to a tropical oasis is

34. **Manoa Falls**—*At the end of Manoa Road, past Paradise Park and Lyon Arboretum.* This one-mile walk ends at a lovely waterfall and fresh-water pool. The trail is frequently muddy

since it's in a forest that receives over 160 inches of rainfall a year, so wear appropriate footwear. Heed the signs and don't attempt to climb above the falls. It's a dangerous area, and many have fallen.

Historic Sites

35. **Aloha Tower**—*Pier 9 at Nimitz Highway.* Built in 1921, Hawaii's version of the Statue of Liberty greets ships arriving in Honolulu Harbor. An observation deck on the tenth floor offers a spectacular view of the harbor, downtown Honolulu, and the coast. The tenth floor also houses the harbor traffic controller's station. If you catch them at the right moment, they sometimes show visitors how they manage the traffic in and out of the busy port. Observation deck open from 8:00am to 9:00pm daily.

36. **Amelia Earhart Memorial**—*Diamond Head Road, Kuilei Cliffs middle lookout.* This site is dedicated to Amelia Earhart, the first woman to fly across the Atlantic Ocean, the first woman to fly solo across the continental U.S., and the first person to fly alone from Hawaii to the Mainland. In 1935, she flew from Wheeler Air Force Base on Oahu to Oakland, CA in 12 hours, 50 minutes. Four years later she attempted to fly from New Guinea to Howland Island, but she never reached her destination and was presumed lost at sea. In the base of the stone monument, a box contains her flight plan and other memorabilia.

   This lookout is a favorite spot for watching the final leg of the Trans-Pacific Yacht Race (in June and July every other year) and the Molokai-to-Oahu Canoe Race in September and October.

Chinatown—*15-block area downtown between Nuuanu and River Streets and Beretania and Nimitz.* Honolulu's Chinatown has a fascinating history, dating back to the early 1800's. Today, it is a colorful blend of ethnic groups selling their wares

The Aloha Tower.

and perpetuating their cultural traditions. Many historic buildings in the area have been renovated recently as part of a Chinatown renaissance. For a more in-depth guide, pick up a copy of *Exploring Honolulu's Chinatown* (Bess Press, PO Box 22388, Honolulu, HI 96822). For a brief visit, the following spots are especially interesting:

37. **Chinatown Cultural Plaza**—100 North Beretaina. The Cultural Plaza contains several shops, restaurants, and a

stage in the center of the courtyard where entertainment is held from time to time. Two of the most interesting spots are the **Sun Yat-sen Hall** and the **United Chinese Press** on the second floor above the Fortune Gate Restaurant. The Hall has a collection of archival photos of Sun Yat-sen and his followers. At the United Chinese Press, you can watch a printer who still sets type by hand for a Chinese newspaper. Arrive before 10:30am to watch him in action.

38. **Izumo Taisha Shrine**—*corner of North Kukui facing the Nuuanu Stream*. Visitors are welcome at this Shinto temple erected in 1923. There are no services on Sundays, but there are usually services on the tenth of each month. It's an ancient Japanese tradition to visit the shrine to give thanks for the blessings of the past and to ask divine guidance and protection for the new year. Remember to remove your shoes before entering.

39. **Kuan Yin Temple**—170 *North Vineyard*. The Kuan Yin Temple, one of the oldest Chinese temples in town, was first built in the 1880's and has been rebuilt several times. It contains one of the most beautiful shrines on the Island. On the center altar is Kuan Yin, Goddess of Mercy. Visitors are welcome, but show respect and don't take flash pictures.

40. **Wo Fat Restaurant**—*Corner of Hotel and Maunakea Streets*. The oldest restaurant in Honolulu, Wo Fat dates back to 1882 but was destroyed twice by the Chinatown fires of 1886 and 1900. The present colorful structure was built in 1937. On the walls inside are numerous archival photos of the early Chinese in Hawaii.

41. **Haleiwa**—*Kamehameha Highway, north shore*. Haleiwa is the most picturesque town on the north shore, and in the late 1800's was the first tourist resort in Hawaii. It's a charming place full of surfers, shave-ice stands, and arty boutiques. An interesting landmark is the **Liliuokalani Church**, 66-090 Kamehameha Highway, named after Hawaii's last reigning

monarch. Inside there's a historic clock which was a gift from the Queen, and you'll notice that instead of numbers on the face, there are letters spelling out the Queen's name. The church is usually open from 6:30am to 1:00pm, except Mondays and Thursdays. Phone: 637-9364.

42. **Hawaii State Capitol**—*Beretania St.* Hawaii's State Capitol is a unique architectural masterpiece which incorporates symbolism of Hawaii's environment. The building is surrounded by a reflecting pool (representing the sea), out of which rise the House and Senate chambers (representing volcanoes). Visitors can arrange a tour of the building in the Sergeant-at-Arms office, Room 036, or by calling 548-7851. The tour lasts about an hour and includes a 30-minute presentation describing the symbolism of the building, an overview of Hawaii's politics, and a visit to the Governor's and Lt. Governor's offices.

43. **Honolulu Hale**—*Corner of King and Punchbowl.* Built in 1929, this beautiful, Spanish-style building houses Honolulu's City Hall, the Mayor's office, the City Council chambers, and a small gallery which has frequent art exhibits. In the Mayor's office on the third floor, visitors can get a booklet which tells more about the building.

44. **Iolani Palace**—*corner of Richards and King Streets.* The only royal palace on American soil, the Iolani Palace housed Hawaiian royalty from 1882 until January 1893, when a group of American businessmen and Marines overthrew Queen Liliuokalani.

There is an admission charge to tour the inside of the Palace, but there's no fee to explore the grounds and see the barracks which served as headquarters for the Royal Guards. The bandstand, built in 1883 for the coronation of King Kalakaua and Queen Kapiolani, is now the site of free concerts by the Royal Hawaiian Band every Friday at noon.

45. **Kamehameha I Statue**—*King Street, across from Iolani Palace.* This black and gold statue is a copy of the original, which sank when the ship carrying it from Europe went down near the Falkland Islands. The original was salvaged and now stands in the town of Kapaau on the Island of Hawaii. On Kamehameha Day, June 11, the figure is draped with 18-foot-long leis. The Judiciary Building behind the statue was built in 1874 and housed the Hawaiian legislature.

46. **U.S.S. Arizona Memorial**—*off Kamehameha Highway past the airport and Hickam Air Force Base. Watch for signs.* The U.S. Navy operates launches that take visitors out to the memorial from 8:00am to 3:00pm daily, except Monday and some holidays. This is a very popular visitor attraction, so it's best to arrive early. Visitors can browse through a museum and bookstore while waiting in line. After watching a 20-minute documentary on the 1941 attack on Pearl Harbor, the launch speeds you to the memorial. The memorial straddles the hull of the U.S.S. Arizona, which still contains the remains of the 1,117 men who died in the attack.

No children under age six are allowed on the launches. Call 422-0561 for more information.

47. **Kawaiahao Church**—*corner of King and Punchbowl Streets.* Sometimes called the "Westminster Abbey of Hawaii," this landmark, Honolulu's oldest church, is on the National Register of Historic Buildings. It was completed in 1841 out of nearly 14,000 coral blocks. Sunday services are conducted in English and Hawaiian at 10:30am, and visitors are invited to tour the church afterwards. Phone: 522-1334. Behind the church is King Lunalilo's Tomb, built in 1876.

48. **Keaiwa Heiau State Park**—*Aiea Heights Drive.* A *heiau* used by *kahunas* (Hawaiian priests), located in this park, contains several plants used for medicinal purposes by the kahunas. The State Parks Division has labeled the plants and maintains the temple. The park also contains the Aiea Loop trail, a 4.8-mile hike through a forest of Norfolk pines, eucalyptus, bamboo, and other flora. This is a favorite hiking trail

The replica statue of Kamehameha I on Oahu.

for families because it is not too strenuous. Open daily from 7:00am to 7:45pm. Phone: 488-6626.

49. **Mormon Temple**—55-600 Naniloa Loop in Laie. This impressive white edifice was built in 1919. Though visitors may not enter the temple, you may tour the grounds and visitor center to learn more about the Mormon Church. Open daily from 9:00am to 8:00pm. Phone: 293-9297.

50. **Natatorium War Memorial**—2815 Kalakaua. This memorial, built in 1927, honors Hawaii's soldiers who died in World War I. At that time it was the country's largest saltwater swimming pool and was designed for Olympic swimming meets and public swimming. The pool is now closed due to deterioration, but a "Save the Natatorium" group has been raising money to restore the memorial.

51. **National Memorial Cemetery of the Pacific**—Punchbowl, 2177 Puowaina Drive. Sometimes called the "Arlington of the Pacific," this cemetery is the resting place for more than 20,000 servicemen who died in World War II, the Korean War, and the Vietnam War. This 112-acre site, visited by more than four million people each year, is the state's top visitor attraction. Ancient Hawaiians called the site Puowaina (Hill of Sacrifice) because human sacrifices were made there.

   The gates are open from 8:00am to 5:00pm daily, and visitors can pick up a descriptive pamphlet in the administration building near the flagpole. Phone: 541-1430.

52. **Puu-o-Mahuka Heiau**—turn off Kamehameha Highway at Pupukea Road and drive up the hill for 0.7 mile to a dirt road which leads to the temple. These ruins of an ancient heiau are the largest on Oahu and are registered as a National Historic Landmark. It is believed that three of Vancouver's crewmen were sacrificed there. From the heiau you get a magnificent view of the North Shore.

The reconstructed heiau in Makaha Valley.

53. **Kaneaki Heiau**—*behind the Sheraton Makaha Resort*, 84-626 Makaha Valley Rd. Visitors can see a reconstructed 15th-century *heiau* (temple) in a lovely spot in Makaha Valley (also home to dozens of peacocks). Open Tuesday through Sunday 10:00am to 2:00pm, weather permitting. Call the hotel's guest services at 695-9511 to be sure it's open before you drive out.

54. **Royal Mausoleum**—2261 Nuuanu Ave. This mausoleum is considered the most sacred burial place in the islands. The three-acre grounds contain a chapel designed in the shape of a cross and a mausoleum with the remains of six of the eight monarchs who ruled over the Hawaiian kingdom: Kamehameha II, III, IV, and V, Kalalaua, and Queen Lili-uokalani. Open Monday through Friday, 8:00am to 4:00pm, except for holidays.

Lectures

55. **The Friday Conversation**—1802 *Keeaumoku* St. The Hawaii Committee for the Humanities sponsors this lecture series on history, literature, philosophy, and cultural heritage. Held the first and third Friday of each month at 4:00pm. No lectures during the summer. Call 732-5402 for information.

Lessons

56. **Coconut Hat Weaving and Frond Sculpture**—*Hilton Hawaiian Village*, 2005 *Kalia Road*. Learn to make interesting and useful hats and other decorative items with coconut fronds Monday, Wednesday, and Friday. Also at the Sheraton-Waikiki Hotel, 2255 Kalakaua at 8:30am. Call 261-1814 for daily schedule.

57. **Chinese Cooking**—*Great Wok of China*, 2233 *Kalakaua*, *3rd floor*, *Building* B. Each Friday at 11:30am, cooks demonstrate how to prepare Oriental dishes, and class participants get to sample the results. Phone: 922-5373.

58. **Ballroom Dancing**—*Waikiki Community Center*, 310 *Paoakalani Ave*. Learn the tango, waltz, foxtrot, and all those other dances you've always wanted to know on Thursdays at 10:00am. Phone: 923-1802.

59. **Hula**—*Royal Hawaiian Shopping Center*, 2201 *Kalakaua*, *Building C*, *3rd floor*. Take lessons from Pua Ke'ala, a graduate of Halau Hula O Maiki on Wednesdays and Fridays at 10:30am. Phone: 922-0588.

60. **Israeli Folk Dance Club**—*Kahala Recreation Center*, 4495 *Pahoa Ave*. This group teaches and demonstrates the folk dances of Israel on Wednesdays at 7:30pm. Phone: 373-2561.

61. **International Folk Dancing**—*Makiki District Park, Keeaumoku St. and Wilder Ave.* Folk dances from around the world are taught and performed on Sundays at 7:30pm. Phone: 536-4049, 946-9143, or 486-0694.

62. **Scottish Country Dancing**—*Moiliili Community Center, 2535 South King, 3rd floor.* Sponsored by the royal Scottish Country Dance Society. Wednesday at 7:00 pm. Phone: 955-1555.

63. **Square Dancing**—*Kapiolani Bandstand.* Swing your partner round and round on Wednesdays at 8:00pm. Phone: 941-1607.

64. **Square Dancing, Part II**—*Kahala Recreation Center, 4495 Pahoa Ave.* Fridays at 7:30pm. Sponsored by Diamond Heads 'N Sides Square Dance Club. Phone: 737-2724.

65. **Coconut Frond Weaving**—*Royal Hawaiian Shopping Center, 2201 Kalakaua, Building A, 3rd floor.* Uncle Harry Kuikahi demonstrates the Hawaiian art of weaving coconut fronds and will teach you to make baskets and other decorative items. Tuesday and Thursday at 9:30am. Phone: 922-0588.

66. **Hawaiian Quilting**—*Royal Hawaiian Shopping Center, 2201 Kalakaua, Building A, 3rd floor.* Auntie Deborah Kakalia demonstrates the art of Hawaiian quilting. Tuesday and Thursday at 9:30am. Phone: 922-0588.

67. **Karate**—*Waikiki Community Center, 310 Paoakalani Ave.* Learn the ancient martial art of karate with lessons on Mondays at 6:30pm. Phone: 923-1802.

68. **Lei-making**—*Royal Hawaiian Shopping Center, 2201 Kalakaua, Building B-C bridgeway, 2nd floor.* Learn how to string flowers together to make lovely leis. Monday and Friday at 11:00am. Phone: 922-0588.

69. **Tai Chi**—*Waikiki Community Center*, 310 Paoakalani. Learn ancient Chinese body and energy control exercises. Wednesday and Friday at 11:00am. Phone: 923-1802.

Museums

70. **Bishop Museum, Planetarium, Telescope, and Science Center**—1525 *Bernice St.* Charles Reed Bishop founded the Bishop Museum in 1889 in memory of his wife Princess Bernice Pauahi Bishop, the last direct descendant of King Kamehameha the Great. Though there's an admission charge for the main part of the museum, there's a free exhibit in the Science Center entitled "The Wayfinding Art," which explores non-instrument navigational techniques used by the ancient Polynesians. On Friday and Saturday evenings, visitors may use a 12-inch telescope, weather permitting. Call the planetarium first at 848-4136. There is also no charge to visit the gift shop, which contains an excellent selection of books on Hawaii and the Pacific.

71. **Damien Museum**—130 *Ohua behind St. Augustine Church in Waikiki*. This museum contains memorabilia from Father Damien's work on Molokai, where he dedicated his life to working with Hansen's Disease (leprosy) patients. A 20-minute video describes his work and the hardships of those banished to Kalaupapa to die. Open Monday through Friday from 9:00am to 3:00pm, and Saturday from 9:00am to noon. Phone: 923-2690.

72. **Pacific Whaling Museum**—*Sea Life Park, Kalanianaole Highway at Makapuu*. Sea Life Park's 62-acre complex houses the Pacific Whaling Museum, which contains the largest collection of whaling artifacts in the Pacific, including a reconstructed skeleton of a sperm whale. There is an admission charge to the main part of Sea Life Park, but you can visit the museum, restaurant, and sea lion pool for free. Open 9:30am to 4:30pm daily. Phone: 259-5177.

73. **U.S. Army Museum at Fort DeRussy**—2055 Kalia Road, Waikiki. This museum, housed inside Battery Randolph, contains artifacts, uniforms, photos, and other memorabilia in a historical display of the U.S. Army's history from the American Revolution to Vietnam. Open daily 10:00am to 4:30pm, except Monday. Phone: 543-2639.

Parks

74. **Kapiolani Park**—Kalakaua Avenue at Monsarrat. This 170-acre area of greenery is one of Honolulu's most popular parks. It offers a jogging path, softball diamond, driving range, archery range, tennis courts, an amphitheater, and a bandstand where music and dance programs are frequently presented. Dedicated in 1877, this was Honolulu's first large public park and was named after Queen Kapiolani, wife of King Kalakaua. At one time the park was also the site of a race track and heavy gambling.

Publications

75. Free visitor publications are available around the island at shopping centers, car rental agencies, hotels, and other distribution points (especially in Waikiki). Look for *Guide to Oahu, Waikiki Beach Press, Spotlight, This Week, Oahu Drive Guide, The Downtown Planet* (downtown only), and *The Beat*. Most of these contain maps, calendars of events, discount coupons, and feature articles about island attractions.

Porpoise & Turtle Pool

76. **Kahala Hilton Porpoise and Turtle Pool**—5000 Kahala Ave. This prestigious hotel has beautifully landscaped grounds with a unique porpoise and turtle pool. Visitors can watch

them being fed at 11:00am, 2:00pm, and 4:00pm. Phone: 734-2211.

Scenic Attractions

77. **Halona Blowhole**—*Kalanianaole Highway, just east of Koko Head (look for the Hawaii Visitors Bureau marker).* Halona Blowhole is a natural lava tube at the base of the cliff which spouts water when a wave hits. There is a small parking lot and lookout deck where you can watch the blowhole and perhaps catch sight of the Island of Molokai, 22 miles across the Kaiwi Channel. Be sure to lock your car, since this is a favorite spot for thieves.

78. **Nuuanu Pali Lookout**—*off Pali Highway (look for sign indicating turnoff).* The Pali offers Oahu's most famous view, a panorama of Windward Oahu. This site, at the peak of 1,000-foot cliffs, was the battleground where Kamehameha I drove Oahu's warriors over the edge and gained domination of the kingdom. Some days such forceful tradewinds blow there that it's difficult to walk.

79. **Tantalus-Round Top Drive**—This drive has one of the most spectacular views of Honolulu. At the top of the mountain, Puu Ualakaa Park is a cool little oasis with a view from Koko Head to the Waianae Mountains. The park closes at dark. A short drive down the mountain from the park is a lookout point which is the best spot for viewing Honolulu at night.

Swimming Pools

80. There are free public swimming pools at the following locations on Oahu:

Aiea Recreation Center—99-350 Aiea Heights Drive, 488-4267.
Booth District Park—2331 Kanealii Ave., 528-3993.

Kailua Recreation Center—21 South Kainalu Dr., 261-4830.
Kaneohe District Park—45-660 Keaahala Rd., 247-3125.
Kanewai Playground—2695 Dole, 734-1264.
Kapaolono Playground—701 11th Ave., 735-7917.
Makakilo—92-665 Anipeahi, 672-3840.
Manana—1550 Kuahaka, 455-2553.
Manoa Valley Recreation Center—2721 Kaaipu Ave., 988-6868.
McCully Recreation Center—831 Pumehana, 947-6070.
Moanalua—1289 Mahiole, 839-9611.
Palolo Recreation Center—2007 Palolo Ave., 737-2486.
Pearl City Recreation Center—785 Hoomaemae, 455-3833.
Wahiawa Recreation Center—1139A Kilani Ave., 621-0857.
Waialua Recreation Center—67-180 Goodale Avenue, 637-6061.
Waipahu Recreation Center—94-230 Paiwa, 671-7911.

Sports

81. **Airplane Gliding**—Dillingham Airfield, Mokuleia. Every day you can watch one- and two-passenger sailplanes ride the air currents and cruise the magnificent Waianae range and coastline. Planes take off from about 10:00am to 5:30pm. Call 623-6711 for more information.

82. **Fencing**—Queen's Surf Beach Pavilion, Waikiki. The Hawaii Fencing Association practices each Sunday at 3:00pm and on Mondays at the Kailua Recreation Center at 6:30pm.

83. **Hang-gliding**—Cliffs above Makapuu, off Kalanianaole Highway. Watch the hang-gliders take off from the 1,200-foot cliffs and soar over Sea Life Park down to the beach at Makapuu.

84. **Honolulu Marathon Clinic**—Kapiolani Park Bandstand. Every Sunday at 7:30am, runners training for the marathon meet at the park and hear an instructional talk about running, then break into groups with different levels of running experience for a run around the park. Call 734-7200 for information.

85. **Surfing**—*North Shore*. Beaches along the North Shore are among the most famous surfing beaches in the world. International surfing championships are held from late November through January when waves reach 15 to 20 feet in height. Sunset, Pipeline, and Waimea offer the most exciting viewing when the surf's up. Call 836-1952 for daily surf reports.

86. **Tennis**—Free public courts are available at the following locations:

Ala Moana Park—1201 Ala Moana Blvd., 10 courts.
Diamond Head Tennis Center—3908 Paki Ave., 7 courts.
Kapiolani Park Tennis Courts—2748 Kalakaua, 4 courts.

Though Oahu has 126 public courts, they are crowded and require a wait. For a complete listing, check with the Hawaii Visitors Bureau for their brochure *Golf and Tennis in Hawaii*. Phone: 923-1811.

Tea Ceremony

87. **Japanese Tea Ceremony**—245 *Saratoga* Rd. The Urasenke Foundation offers an opportunity to learn about *Chado* (the Way of Tea) through demonstrations and discussions held Wednesday and Friday at 10:00am. The tea ceremony provides an intriguing insight into Japanese culture, encompassing etiquette, philosophy, arts and crafts, ceramics, architecture, and landscaping. Reservations are recommended. Phone: 923-3059.

University of Hawaii

88. **The University of Hawaii** sits on 300 acres in Manoa Valley and has two major libraries, two art galleries, a swimming pool, frequent concerts and lectures, and numerous other free activities going on all the time. The campus also has over 500 varieties of tropical and subtropical flora, which

are described in a publication entitled *Campus Plants*. Ask for a copy at the libraries or Hawaii Hall, room 2.

89. **The East-West Center**, which shares part of the University campus, is a federally-funded project designed to promote mutual understanding among the peoples of Asia, the Pacific, and the U.S. The Center offers a tour on Tuesday, Wednesday, and Thursday at 1:30pm which includes a video about the center's activities. Meet in Jefferson Hall, 1777 East-West Road, garden level. Reservations are not necessary for groups of fewer than 10. Call 944-7691 for more information.

Zoo

90. **Honolulu Zoo**—151 *Kapahulu Ave.* The zoo normally charges a $1.00 admission fee, but during the summer months they have the free "Wildest Show in Town" on Wednesday evenings. The event begins after the zoo's regular closing time of 4:00pm, and there is a show at 6:00pm on the stage in the main courtyard. Families can bring a picnic supper and enjoy a variety of performances, including ballet, choirs, puppet shows, and other entertainers. Held during June, July, and August only. Call 926-6982.

Oahu Annual Events

January
91. **Health & Fitness Fair**—*Blaisdell Exhibition Hall, 777 Ward Ave.* Hundreds of exhibitors show off their health- and fitness-related products and ideas. For dates and hours, call 523-7755.

February
92. **Punahou Carnival**—*Corner of Wilder and Punahou Streets.* The Punahou School sponsors a carnival with rides, food, crafts, entertainment, and more, on the first Friday and Saturday

of each February. There is no charge to enter and watch the festivities. Phone: 944-5711.

March

93. **Prince Kuhio Day**—*Iolani Palace, corner of King and Richards Streets; and Royal Mausoleum, 2261 Nuuanu Ave.* March 26 is Prince Kuhio Day in Hawaii, and there are ceremonies at Iolani Palace and later at his tomb at the Royal Mausoleum.

April

94. **Iolani Carnival**—*563 Kamoku.* This annual carnival features homemade foods, crafts, games, rides, and other activities. Call 949-5355 for dates.

95. **Jazz Festival**—*Leeward Community College, 96-045 Ala Ike.* Hear the best Island jazz musicians at this annual outdoor concert on the grounds of the Leeward Community College. Call 455-0011.

June

96. **Kamehameha Day**—*Island-wide.* There is a parade downtown and festivities around the island during this holiday to honor King Kamehameha. The holiday is June 11, but the activities sometimes fall on different days. Watch local papers.

97. **Mission Houses Craft Fair**—*553 South King St.* The Mission Houses Museum usually hosts a wonderful arts and crafts fair around Kamehameha Day. This is an excellent opportunity to see works by many of the Island's best craftsmen.

July

98. **Pacific Handcrafters Guild Craft Fair**—*Thomas Square, between King and Beretania at Ward.* Fine quality arts and crafts are displayed at this annual fair, along with craft demonstrations, ethnic foods, and entertainment. Call 538-7227 for exact dates.

99. **July 4th Parade**—*Kainalu Drive, Kailua*. Called the "largest 4th of July Parade in the Pacific," this parade begins at the intersection of Kainalu Drive and North Kalaheo around 10:00am. A reviewing stand at St. Christopher's Church, 93 N. Kainalu Drive, is a good place to watch the action. Call 261-2727 for more information.

100. **Prince Lot Hula Festival**—*Moanalua Gardens, off* H-1 *Highway*. Prince Lot maintained a home on the site of what is now Moanalua Gardens. He was especially devoted to maintaining the ancient Hawaiian dances, and the Moanalua Gardens Foundation honors the former monarch each year in this hula festival in which several *halau* (schools) share their different styles and interpretations of hula. There are also arts and crafts displays, demonstrations, and food booths. Call 839-5334 for exact date.

101. **Ukulele Festival**—*Kapiolani Park Bandstand*. Several hundred performers participate in the annual Ukulele Festival, which begins around 1:00pm at the Kapiolani Park Bandstand. Take a picnic and enjoy the afternoon concert, which includes neophytes as well as professionals. Call 737-3739 for more information.

August

102. **Na Hula O Hawaii**—*Kapiolani Park Bandstand*. The Kalama Hawaiiana unit of Honolulu's Parks and Recreation Dept. ends their "Summer Fun" program with this dance festival featuring graduates of all ages from the program's hula classes and several hula *halau*. Call 262-2396 for dates and times.

September

103. **Aloha Week**—*Island-wide events*. During Aloha Week there are canoe races, street parties, parades, and many other activities, most of which are free. Call 944-8857 for dates.

104. **Okinawan Festival**—*Thomas Square.* This festival honors Hawaii's people of Okinawan heritage with dances, arts and crafts exhibits, demonstrations, and other events. Call 546-8119.

December

105. **Billabong Pro-Coors Triple Crown of Surfing**—*Sunset Beach.* The actual date of this event depends on surf conditions, but it's an opportunity to see the pros in action riding some of Oahu's big waves. Phone: 737-3313.

106. **Handel's Messiah**—*Central Union Church,* 1660 *South Beretania.* The first Sunday of Advent, a 100-voice choir is featured in an hour-long concert that has been performed for over 70 years by the Central Union Church. Call 941-0957.

107. **Hawaii International Film Festival**—*various theaters around the island.* The East-West Center sponsors this annual event which includes feature films, shorts, documentaries, special lectures, and workshops during a week-long festival. Call 944-7111 for a schedule of the events and exact dates.

108. **Honolulu Marathon**—*Aloha Tower.* Thousands of runners join this 26-mile run from the Aloha Tower to Hawaii Kai and back to Kapiolani Park. The best place to watch is near the finish line in Kapiolani Park. Call 734-7200 for date.

109. **Pacific Handcrafters Guild Christmas Fair**—*Thomas Square.* These are the same folks who sponsor the craft fair in July. They usually have more displays right before Christmas. Phone: 538-7227.

Island
of
Maui

*M*aui, the second largest of the Hawaiian islands, is nicknamed the "Valley Isle" because of its shape. The island was once two separate volcanic peaks which eventually fused together.

Hawaii offers a spectacular diversity of geologic formations, including active volcanoes, jagged canyons, moon-like craters, and snowcapped mountains. Maui's most impressive sight is Haleakala Crater, a depression large enough to hold all of Manhattan. Haleakala, rising over 10,000 feet above sea level, has 30 miles of hiking and riding trails, and visitors can inspect cinder cones, lava tubes, and spatter vents. Haleakala also contains Science City, a complex that houses huge telescopes used to track satellites across the sky.

This area is also home to one of the rarest birds in the world, the nene. At one time, over 25,000 of these wild geese lived on the islands of Maui and Hawaii. But westerners arrived and decided they were good to eat. Today, scientists are trying desperately to save the nene from extinction.

Drive along Honoopiilani Highway from December through May, and you may catch sight of Maui's most exciting visitors, the humpback whales. Every year these huge, gentle mammals journey from Alaska to mate and give birth in the warm waters off Maui. At one time the humpbacks numbered about 15,000; fewer than 1,000 remain today.

History buffs will love the quaint old town of Lahaina, which has retained the flavor of its past as a port for rowdy whalers. The Lahaina Restoration Foundation has worked hard to preserve the town, now on the National Register of Historic Places.

The drive along Route 36 takes you to "heavenly" Hana, an area originally settled by the Marquesans about 500A.D. The 52-mile road to Hana is famous for its twists and turns through an incredibly scenic area of waterfalls, pools, and verdant countryside.

Hana, Haleakala, and Lahaina are just a few of the attractions on this island which make people say "Maui no ka oi" — "Maui is the best."

Art

110. **Dolphin Gallery**—Whalers Village in Kaanapali and Front Street in Lahaina. A marine art gallery featuring a collection of glass, bronze, and wood sculptures, plus oils, watercolors, and jewelry. Open daily 9:00am to 10:00pm. Phone: 661-5115.

111. **Grycner Gallery**—758 Front St., Lahaina. This gallery is the exclusive representative of Miguel Martinez and Navajo artist R. C. Gorman. Open Monday to Saturday 9:00am to 10:00pm. Phone: 667-9112.

112. **Hui Noeau Visual Arts Center**—2841 Baldwin Ave., Makawao. This non-profit educational and cultural organization is located in the old Baldwin estate, Kaluanui, and offers film and slide presentations and lectures in addition to regular exhibitions. Open daily 9:00am to 3:00pm. Phone: 572-6560.

113. **Lahaina Arts Society**—649 Wharf St., Lahaina. This society of Maui artists, housed in the historic courthouse at the Lahaina Harbor, has exhibits in their main gallery and in the Old Jail Gallery in the courthouse basement, which also has a permanent exhibit of historic photos of Lahaina and the surrounding area. The Courthouse gallery has bi-monthly shows, and the Old Jail Gallery's shows change monthly. The Society also sponsors the "art under the banyan tree" exhibit across the street from the Pioneer

" *art under the banyan tree*" *Sat - Sun   10:00 - 4:00*

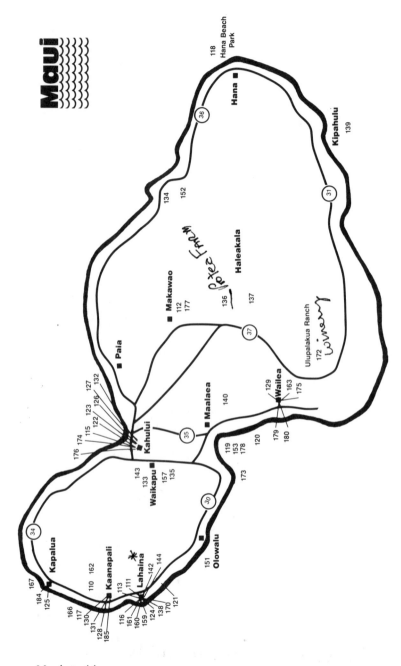

Maui • 44

Inn on Saturdays, Sundays, and holidays from 10:00am to 4:00pm. Both galleries are open daily from 10:00am to 4:00pm. Phone: 661-0111.

114. **Maui Crafts Guild**—43 Hana Highway, Paia. The Guild displays a variety of handcrafted items by Maui artisans, including ceramics, porcelain, koa wood sculptures, blown glass, fiber arts, and other items. Phone: 579-9697.

115. **Magic Moments Gallery**—333 Dairy Road, Kahului. This new gallery is the only one on Maui devoted entirely to photography, featuring works by Lani Churchill, Randy Hufford, and Ed Robinson. Open Monday to Friday 8:00am to 4:00pm. Phone: 871-5806.

116. **Old Lahaina Luau Gallery**—505 Front St., Lahaina. This gallery features fine arts and Hawaiian crafts including koa and milo woodwork and Hawaiian quilting. Open Monday through Saturday, 9:00am to 9:00pm, Sunday 9:00am to 6:00pm. Phone: 667-1998.

Beach Parks

117. **Hanaka'o'o Beach Park**—*begins at the end of* Wahikuli State Park *and runs to* Black Rock. This beach has park facilities and good swimming, and is the site of canoe races in the summer.

118. **Hana Beach Park**—Hana. A local favorite, Hana has the safest swimming beach in East Maui.

119. **Kalama Beach Park**—*in* Kihei. This 36-acre park has a variety of recreational and picnic facilities, including a volleyball and basketball court and a safe swimming beach.

120. **Kamaole Beach Park I, II, and III**—*in Kihei bordering South Kihei Road.* These beaches are Kihei's most popular. All have restrooms, picnic facilities, and good swimming areas.

121. **Launiupoko State Wayside Park**—*2.5 miles south of Lahaina.* This popular park offers views of the neighbor islands of Molokai, Lanai, and Kahoolawe, plus the usual park facilities.

View of Lana', etc.

Tours

122. **Pacific Brewery**—*Imi Kala St., on the grounds of the Old Wailuku Sugar Mill in Wailuku.* Pacific Brewery offers 15-minute tours of their plant from 9:00am to 3:00pm weekdays. The tour reveals how beer is brewed and bottled, and it culminates in a taste test of their Maui Lager. Phone: 244-0396.

123. **Hawaiian Alii Coral Factory**—*Airport Road, Kahului.* At this factory tour, you can watch craftsmen fashion beautiful coral jewelry from pink, red, black, and golden fern coral. There's also a 10-minute video on black coral harvesting, and a free gift to visitors. They provide free transportation to and from hotels and the airport. Phone: 877-7620.

Entertainment

124. **Aloha Friday at the Wharf**—*658 Front St., Lahaina.* Dances and songs of Polynesia are performed by the Maukaukau Hula Halau, Fridays at 6:30pm, on the center stage.

125. **Hula Kahiko O Hawaii**—*The Kapalua Shops in the Kapalua Bay Hotel, Kapalua.* Ancient hula of Hawaii is performed every Thursday at 10:00am by kumu hula Cliff Ahue and

his Hula Halau Ho'oulu o Ka'ula, with stories by Maui County historian Inez Ashdown. Located in the shopping center's garden courtyard.

126. **Maui Mall**—70 East *Kaahumanu Ave., Kahului*. The mall offers entertainment every Saturday at 1:00pm, including a variety of dancers, singers, and entertainers.

127. **Open Mike Night**—*The Artful Dodger, 55 Kaahumanu Ave., Kahului*. Professionals and amateurs share their music, poetry, drama, and humor every Tuesday evening from 7:00pm to 9:30pm. Phone: 871-2677.

128. **Pau Hana Show**—*Hyatt Regency Maui, Kaanapali*. The Hyatt celebrates the end of the work week with Hawaiian arts and crafts in the Atrium Lobby from 10:30am to 3:00pm Fridays, including Hawaiian quilting, lei-making, and other crafts. At 3:00pm, the activities continue in the Pavillion Restaurant with a Hawaiian music and dance revue.

129. **Polynesian Entertainment**—*Wailea Shopping Village, Wailea*. A Polynesian revue on the Village Green, Tuesdays at 1:30pm.

130. **Polynesian Show**—*Whaler's Village in Kaanapali*. Every Thursday through Saturday at 5:30pm, dancers dressed in traditional costumes perform a variety of Polynesian dances while musicians accompany them with traditional instruments. The Thursday and Friday performances are held on the center's lower-level stage, and the Saturday show is enacted right on the beach.

131. **Torchlighting Ceremony and Cliff Dive**—*Sheraton Maui, Kaanapali*. A local in native dress appears just before sunset with a burning torch and lights a line of tiki torches along the Black Rock promontory. He then casts his lei into the waves and plunges off the cliff into the sea in a re-enactment of an ancient ritual. Legend says that warriors leapt from Black Rock to join the spirit world. You can watch from the hotel bar by the pool.

132. **Maui Chess Club**—*The Artful Dodger*, 55 *Kaahumanu Ave.*, *Kahului*. Beginners and intermediate players can get instruction and then play with the club on Mondays beginning at 6:30pm. Call 579-9623 or 871-2677.

Gardens

133. **The Heritage Garden/Kepaniwai Park**—*Iao Valley Road*. This state park features pavilions and gardens representative of the different cultures found in Hawaii. It was here in 1790 that King Kamehameha the Great defeated the Mauians in a bloody battle. *Kepaniwai* ("Damming of the Waters") refers to the bodies of slain warriors which blocked the Iao stream. The park also contains picnic tables and barbeque grills.

134. **Keanae Arboretum**—*Hana Highway, about halfway to Hana*. This arboretum contains native Hawaiian plants and introduced trees labeled for a self-guided tour through two miles of hiking trails. Many varieties of taro are planted in the traditional Hawaiian manner.

135. **Maui Tropical Plantation**—*Honoapiilani Highway, Waikapu*. Here you can view an impressive array of Hawaii's crops, including flowers, fruits, vegetables, and nuts. Fifty acres have been planted with sugar cane, bananas, guava, and other island produce, and there's a 10-acre visitor center with exhibits demonstrating the process crops undergo for commercial development. There is a $5 charge to ride a train through the grounds, but the ride is optional. Daily 9:00am to 5:00pm. Phone: 244-7643.

136. **Sunrise Protea Farm**—*Highway* 378 *on the slopes of Haleakala, corner of Ponimoi Place*. This garden has a variety of exotic protea plants which grow well at this altitude. Inside, a crafts center displays dried arrangements, cards, and other items made using protea. This is a good spot to photograph these beautiful plants. Daily 8:00am to 4:00pm. Phone: 878-2119.

137. **University of Hawaii**—*Copp Road off Rte.* 37. This 20-acre experimental station of the Univ. of Hawaii contains protea, roses, and other flowers and vegetables. The office will provide a self-guided tour map. Open Monday through Friday from 8:00am to 3:30pm. Phone: 878-1213.

Garment Factory Tour

138. **Hilo Hattie**—1000 L*imahana Place, Lahaina.* This company offers tours of its factory where muumuus, aloha shirts, swimwear, and other Island fashions are created. The tour includes a lei, refreshments, and free transportation from hotels in Kaanapali and Lahaina. Open daily from 8:30am to 5:00pm. Call 661-8457 for times of hotel pickups.

Hikes

139. **Oheo Gulch/Seven Pools**—*In Kipahulu, Highway* 36. National park rangers lead a four-hour hike from the Oheo Gulch parking lot through the remote Kipahulu Valley, with an opportunity to view both Makahiku Falls and the 384-foot Waimoku Falls. Saturdays at 9:00am. Bring lunch and water. Phone: 572-9306.

Historic Sites

140. **David Malo Memorial Church**—*South of the Maui Lu Resort in Kihei (look for the blue and white shield sign of the Episcopal Church).* This church was built in 1853 after the death of David Malo, a Hawaiian scholar and minister. Church services are still conducted there Sundays at 9:00am.

141. **Halekii and Pihana Heiaus**—*located on Hea Place, Kahului.* These *heiaus* (temples) were used from 1765 to 1895, and legends say they were built by the *menehune*, Hawaii's little people.

Kaahumanu Church, Maui's oldest church.

142. **Jodo Mission Cultural Park**—*off Front St. on Ala Moana St., Lahaina*. In the center of this serene park is a 3.5-ton Buddha, the largest outside of Japan, built to commemorate the arrival of the first Japanese immigrants in 1868. The park includes a temple shrine, crematorium, graveyard, and an outdoor meeting area.

143. **Kaahumanu Church**—*corner Main and High St., Wailuku*. This is the oldest existing church on Maui and the site where Queen Kaahumanu worshipped in a grass shack. The present structure was built in 1876. A 9:00am service is conducted on Sundays with music and prayer in Hawaiian. Phone: 879-4693.

Walking Tour

144. **Lahaina Walking Tour**—*Front St. in Lahaina*. This old whaling town is one of the most popular and picturesque places in Hawaii. The Lahaina Restoration Foundation has worked hard to maintain the town's historic flavor and to restore many of the old buildings in the area. Pick up a free copy of the Lahaina Historical Guide at one of the many distribution spots around town and follow the maps keyed to 31 historical sites in town. The sites are marked by signs posted by the Lahaina Restoration Foundation. There is an admission charge to tour the inside of some of the buildings, but the walking tour is free. A selection of a few of the most interesting sites follows:

145. **Banyan Tree**—*site #9, Front St*. This incredible tree is supposed to be the largest banyan in Hawaii. It takes up over half an acre. The tree was planted in 1873 in memory of the 50th anniversary of the founding of the first Christian mission in Lahaina. On weekends, it shelters the Lahaina Art Society's art show.

146. **Carthaginian**—*site #7, on the waterfront behind the Pioneer Inn.* This replica of a 19th-century brig is the only authentically restored brig in the world. It is typical of the ships that brought the first missionaries to Hawaii. There is an admission charge to go on board.

147. **Hale Pa'i**—*site #28, Lahainaluna Road.* This printing house of Lahainaluna Seminary was founded by Protestant missionaries in 1831 and produced thousands of pages of educational materials in Hawaiian. The school is the oldest educational institution west of the Rockies. Open Monday through Saturday, 9:00am to 4:00pm.

148. **Pioneer Inn**—*site #8.* This quaint old hotel was built in 1901 and renovated in 1964. It has been featured in several movies and contains an impressive collection of whaling artifacts and memorabilia. The hotel is still in business today, and the bar downstairs evokes the memory of the old whaling days.

149. **The Old Prison**—*site #21, corner of Waine'e and Prison St.* This old building, Hale Pa'ahao, was used to lock up sailors who didn't return to their ships at sunset, or for drunkenness and dangerous horseriding. It's now used for community gatherings.

150. **Waine'e Church and Cemetery**—*site #17-18.* The first stone church in the islands, Waine'e was built between 1828 and 1832 for the Protestant mission. It has been burned and blown down several times, but always rebuilt. The cemetery next to the church is the final resting place of many important Hawaiians, including Keopuolani, the wife of Kamehameha I, and Kaumuali'i, chief of Kauai.

More Historic Sites

151. **Olowalu Petroglyphs**—5 *miles southeast of* Lahaina *on* Highway 30, *behind Olowalu General Store and one-half mile past the water tower.* You have to do a bit of climbing to see these 300-year old rock carvings by early Hawaiians. Look for the remains of an old wooden stairway.

152. **St. Gabriel's Mission**—*past* Keanae *on* Wailea Road. This picturesque mission was the first Catholic church in the area.

153. **Vancouver Memorial**—*in* Kihei, *across from the* Maui Lu Resort, 575 South Kihei Road. This monument honors Canadian explorer Capt. George Vancouver as the person who "fathered contemporary Maui through his visits to this shore in 1792-1794." The monument was designed and installed by the original owner of the Maui Lu Resort, Gordon Gibson.

Lectures

154. **Pacific Whale Foundation**—During whale season (November-May), the foundation offers weekly presentations on humpback whales, featuring guest speakers who are experts in mammalogy. Mondays, 7:00pm, Westin Hotel; Tuesdays, 7:30pm, Stouffer Wailea Beach Hotel; Wednesdays, 7:00pm at Kaanapali Shores. Call 879-8811 for more information about topics, places, and times.

155. **Save the Whales/Earthtrust** presents films and guest speakers lecturing about whales and dolphins at a variety of locations, including the Whalers Village Museum. Call 661-8755 for dates and times.

The Olowalu petroglyphs near Lahaina. (Photo: Hawaii Visitors Bureau)

Lessons

156. **Lei-making**—*Baldwin House Garden in Lahaina.* Sponsored by the Lahaina Restoration Foundation and the Lahaina Association for Retired People. Thursdays from 10:00am to 4:00pm. Call 661-3262 for more information.

157. **Square Dancing**—*Waikapu Community Center.* Wednesdays at 7:30pm. Phone: 244-0440.

Museums

158. **Hale Pa'i (Printing House)**—*Lahainaluna Road.* (See *Lahaina Walking Tour,* above.)

159. **Lahaina Whaling Museum**—865 *Front St., Lahaina (inside Crazy Shirts).* Rick Ralston, owner of Crazy Shirts, displays a fascinating collection of over 800 whaling artifacts, including harpoons, carved ivory, drawings, miniature replicas of whaling ships, and many other antiques. Open daily 9:00am to 10:00pm. Phone: 661-4775.

160. **Molokai Lens and Lighthouse Exhibit**—*behind Spring House, The Wharf Shopping Center, Front St., Lahaina.* Once the brighest light in the Pacific, this lens was installed in a 132-foot lighthouse at Kalaupapa on Molokai in 1909. With a 1,000-watt bulb, it was visible 21 miles at sea. This huge device, known as a Fresnel lens, contains 26 separate components of lead crystal and bronze fabricated in France and weighs nearly 5,000 pounds.

161. **Surf Museum**—845 *Front St., inside Hobie Sports at the Lahaina Cannery.* Hobie Sports claims to display the world's largest collection of historic surfboards in an exhibit that traces the evolution of surfboards from solid redwood to fly-weight polyurethane vehicles. Open daily 9:30am to 9:30pm. Phone: 661-5777.

162. **Whalers Village Museum**—*Whalers Village, 3rd floor of Building G*. At the entrance to Whalers Village, there's a Whale Pavilion with a 40-foot sperm whale skeleton and ceramic scale models of more than 20 species of whales and dolphins. The rest of the museum is on the 3rd floor, where you can discover 19th-century Maui in one of the finest whaling museums in the Pacific. There's a large collection of sea chests, harpoons, sailor's journals, tools, and artifacts, as well as films, murals, and guided tours. Call 661-5992 for tour times and days.

Movies

163. **Wailea Shopping Village** has a free outdoor movie every Wednesday at 8:00pm. Bring beachmats or chairs. Call 879-4474 for info.

Publications

164. Free visitor literature is available all around the island at shopping centers, car rental agencies, hotels, and other distribution points. *Maui Island Guide, Maui Beach Press, Maui Gold, This Week,* and *Drive Guide* all offer maps, discount coupons, calendars of events, and other tips for visitors.

Scenic Attractions

165. **Iao Needle**—*three miles west of Wailuku*. Mark Twain called this natural wonder the "Yosemite of the Pacific." The Iao Needle is a 2,250-foot product of volcanic erosion that sits amidst the mountains of Puu Kukui and serves as a monument to the Maui soldiers who died in battle with Kamehameha the Great in 1790. There is a picnic area and an easy hiking trail along a stream. This is a major visitor attraction, so don't leave valuables in the car.

The Iao Needle, called the "Yosemite of the Pacific." (Photo: Hawaii Visitors Bureau)

Snorkeling

166. **Black Rock**—*at the Sheraton Hotel in Kaanapali.* This is a good spot for beginners, with many colorful, tame fish that will eat bread from your hand.

167. **Honolua Bay**—*off Highway 30 in West Maui.* This bay has interesting coral formations on the left and right sides.

168. **Ahihi Bay**—*off Makena Road at Makena Beach.* Ahihi is a reserve area, so nothing can be taken from the water. There are no facilities there, just good snorkeling on calm days.

Star Gazing Tour

169. **"Reach Out to the Stars"** —*Hyatt Regency Maui, Kaanapali.* Astronomy buffs can view the night sky from the rooftop of the Lahaina Tower of the Hyatt. Tour includes a slide show of constellations, observation with giant binoculars, and use of a deep space telescope. Wednesday through Sunday at 8:00pm and 9:00pm. Phone: 667-7474, ext. 3206.

nite time

Transportation

170. **Lahaina Express**—*between Kaanapali and Lahaina.* This free shuttle makes pick-ups daily starting at 9:00am at all hotels in the Kaanapali Resort and deposits people at the Banyan Tree Square in Lahaina. The last shuttle returns from the square at 5:00pm. The guest relations desks at the hotels can provide more information about schedules and pick-up sites, or call 661-8748.

Tennis

171. Maui offers the following public tennis courts:

Hana—Hana Ball Park
Kahului—Kahului Community Center
Kihei—Kalama Park
Kihei—fronting Maui Pacific Shores
Lahaina—Lahaina Civic Center
Lahaina—Malu ulu olele Park
Makawao—Eddie Tam Memorial Center
Pukalani—Pukalani Community Center
Wailuku—Maui Community College (after school hours),
   phone: 244-9181
Wailuku—Wailuku Community Center
Wailuku—Wailuku War Memorial

For more information, call the Dept. of Parks & Recreation at 244-9018.

Wine Tasting

172. **Tedeschi Winery Tasting Room**—*at Ulupalakua Ranch, 10 miles past the junction of Highways 377 and 37, on Highway 37.* The tasting room, in an old jail built in 1856, offers samples of Tedeschi's Maui Blanc (produced from pineapple), Maui Blush, and Maui Brut Champagne. This winery was once part of the estate of Capt. James Makee, an American whaler who settled on Maui in the mid-1850s. The drive there is well worth the effort for the spectacular view of upcountry Maui. The tasting room is open from 9:00am to 5:00pm Monday through Friday, and Saturday and Sunday from 10:00am to 5:00pm. Phone: 878-6058.

One of Maui's largest visitors. (Photo: Ed Robinson/Hawaiian Watercolors)

Whale-watching

173. December through May is prime **whale-watching** season off the coast of Maui. The stretch of shoreline along Highway 30 between Lahaina and Maalaea is one of the best observation areas for catching sight of one of these exciting creatures. The Pali Lookout near Maalaea Harbor, an excellent spot, frequently has someone from the Save the Whales organization who can provide information. You can also stop by their office in Lahaina at 930 Wainee St. for brochures and information, or call them at 661-8755.

The Pacific Whale Foundation has a Whale Hotline, 879-4253, which you can call for information. Their office in Kihei at the Kealia Beach Plaza also provides literature.

Zoo

174. **Maui Zoological and Botanical Gardens**—*in Kahului on Kanaloa St., off Kaahumanu.* This is a small zoo with donkeys, sheep, goats, monkeys, and birds. The park, which contains over 150 species of Hawaiian plants, is a good spot to take the kids for a picnic. Open 9:00am to 4:00pm daily.

Maui Annual Events

February

175. **Maui Marine Art Expo**—*Maui Inter-Continental Wailea.* This annual show features over 400 multi-media works by internationally-known marine artists, who also present talks and demonstrations. Open daily from 9:00am to 9:00pm for about two months. Phone: 879-1922.

March

176. **Maui Marathon**—*Kahului.* Hawaii's oldest marathon starts in Kahului at 5:00am and finishes 26.2 miles away in Kaanapali. Call 877-5827 for exact date. There is a fee to enter, but not to watch. There is also a Runners Hotline for up-to-date information about all Maui race events: 242-6042.

177. **Art Maui**—*Makawao, in the old Baldwin home.* Some of Maui's finest artists are featured in this annual juried show in the Hui Noeau Visual Arts Center. Call 878-1568 for dates.

April

178. **Whale Day**—*Kalama Park in Kihei.* This celebration, sponsored by the Pacific Whale Foundation, includes a 10K run, a volleyball tournament, live entertainment, and food in a day of homage to Maui's largest visitors, the humpback whales. Call 879-8811 for more information.

May

179. **May Day**—*Maui Inter-Continental Wailea.* The May Day Lei Contest showcases over 75 beautiful examples of Maui-made leis which are displayed in the hotel's lobby. There is also Hawaiian entertainment, Maui's Royal Court, an

art exhibit, and other festivities. Call 879-1922 for more information.

180. **Valley Isle Triathlon**—*Wailea*. This grueling competition combines running, cycling, and swimming in a race beginning at 6:30am in Wailea. Call 242-6042 for exact date. There is a fee to enter, but not to watch.

June

181. **King Kamehameha Day**—*Lahaina*. Kamehameha Day, a state holiday, is celebrated on Maui with a parade in Lahaina and a *ho'olaulea* (street party) at the Maui Marriott. There are usually other festivities around the island which are announced in the local paper. For information about the parade call 572-7772; about the party call 667-1200.

street party

August

182. **Queen Kaahumanu Canoe Race**—*Kahului Harbor*. Called the ''Iron Woman'' event, this canoe race includes the island's top canoe teams and begins in Kahului Harbor at 8:00am.

September

183. **Aloha Week**—*throughout the island*. Parades, street parties, singing, dancing, and other activities are held at various sites around the island during Aloha Week. Watch the local paper for exact dates and locations or call 944-8857 on Oahu.

November

184. **The World Cup of Golf**—*Kapalua Resort*. One of Maui's finest resorts plays host to world-class golf in an international tournament. Call 669-8233.

185. **Na Mele O Maui**—*Kaanapali*. This celebration of Hawaiian music has been held for over 15 years. Activities include a school song contest, a hula festival, and *ho'olaulea*. Call 661-3271 for dates and locations.

Island
of
Hawaii

*T*he Island of Hawaii, known locally as the Big Island, is the youngest and largest of the Hawaiian Islands. It's also an island of striking contrasts, ranging from snowcapped mountain slopes, to desolate fields of hard, black lava, to serene beaches of white, black, and green sand. (The green beach was formed when a cinder cone of olivine collapsed into the bay, creating sand of tiny olivine pebbles. The black sand beach was formed when hot lava hardened and exploded after hitting the cold ocean waters.)

The Hilo side of the island is home to the state's largest orchid collection, the country's only rainforest zoo, and the world's largest macadamia nut farm. Up north, the rolling pastures contain Hawaii's cowboys, the *paniolos*, most of whom run cattle for Parker Ranch, the largest privately-owned ranch in America.

Along the west coast, the Kailua-Kona area is a favorite with sport fisherman and the site of the annual International Billfish Tournament.

Below Kailua-Kona is Kealakekua Bay, a lovely marine preserve with the best snorkeling on the island—and the site of the murder of Captain Cook. Coffee farms bordering the bay produce Kona coffee, a brew relished by coffee connoisseurs around the world.

The Big Island's most frequently visited attraction is Volcanoes National Park, where visitors can watch an active volcano spewing lava, visit a tree fern jungle, inspect a lava tube, and explore hiking trails throughout the park.

One of the island's greatest adventures is the journey up Mauna Kea, the highest point in the Northern Hemisphere. The giant telescopes at the peak belong to Canada, France, Great Britain, the United States, and the University of Hawaii. One night a week, visitors can tour the observatory and peer through the telescope at a stunningly clear sky.

During the winter, believe it or not, you can ski Mauna Kea. Though there are no chair lifts, skiers are pulled up the mountain behind four-wheel drive vehicles. Many think it's worth it just to say they've "skied Hawaii."

Art

186. **Akona Kai Gallery**—*Kailua-Kona, across from Kailua Pier.* This gallery features hand-blown glass, copper and brass works, and other locally hand-crafted gifts and artwork. Open 9:00am to 6:00pm. Phone: 329-6377.

187. **Gallery of Great Things**—*Highway 19 on the village Green, Waimea.* This gallery specializes in art and artifacts of Hawaii and the South Pacific. Open Monday through Saturday from 9:00am to 5:00pm. Phone: 885-6171.

188. **Kona Arts & Crafts Gallery**—*Kailua-Kona, across from seawall.* Features unusual made-in-Hawaii arts and crafts, including banana bark art, koa carvings, volcano jewelry, and more. Open 9:00am to 9:00pm daily. Phone: 329-5590.

189. **Mauna Loa Art Guild & Gallery**—*Captain Cook on Mamalahoa Highway.* Displays a collection of art including watercolors, pottery, basketry, and glass sculptures. Open Monday through Saturday 10:00am to 6:00pm. Phone: 323-3622.

190. **The Potter's Gallery**—*95 Waianuenue Ave., Hilo.* Features jewelry, raku, pottery, woodwork, baskets, and other crafts by local artisans. They also have a new exhibit every

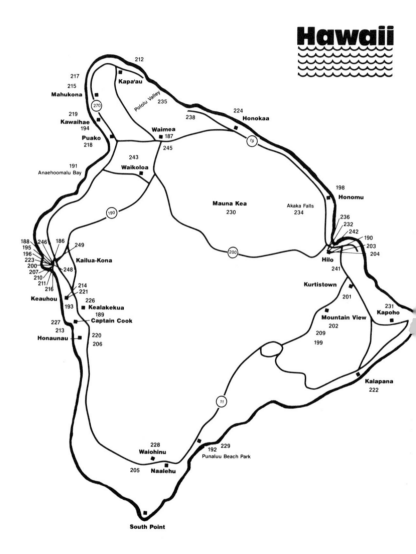

Hawaii

212

217
215
Mahukona

Kapa'au

219
Kawaihae
194

270

Pololu Valley

235

Waimea
187

238

224 Honokaa

19

Puako
218

245

243
Waikoloa

191
Anaehoomalu Bay

198
Honomu

190

Mauna Kea
230

Akaka Falls
234

236
232
242
190
203
204

188
195
196
223
200
207
210
211
216

246
248

186
249

Kailua-Kona

200

Hilo
241

Keauhou

214
221

226
193

189

Kealakekua

Captain Cook

Kurtistown

201

231
Kapoho

227
213
Honaunau

220
206

Mountain View
202

209
199

11

Kalapana
222

228
Waiohinu

192 229
Punaluu Beach Park

205 Naalehu

South Point

month. Open 9:00am to 5:00pm Monday through Saturday. Phone: 935-4069.

Beaches

191. **Anaehoomalu Bay**—5 *miles past* Puako *on* Highway 19. This
beautiful beach fronts the Sheraton Royal Waikoloa Hotel
and is the former site of an ancient fishpond. Several
petroglyph fields and other historic sites are nearby.

192. **Black Sand Beach**—Punaluu Beach Park, *off* Highway 11. This
world-famous beach was created when hot lava reached
the cool waters of the ocean, causing the lava to harden,
shatter into tiny pieces, and become "black sand." This
is a good spot for camping, swimming, body surfing, and
fishing.

193. **Disappearing Beach**—3 *miles south of* Kailua-Kona. This
beach "disappears" occasionally when the sand washes
out to sea, leaving only a lava shoreline. Since there are
dangerous currents there, it's not good for swimming.

194. **Spencer Beach Park**—*off* Highway 270, *near* Kawaihae. This
popular white sand beach is excellent for fishing, swimming, snorkeling, body surfing, and camping. Pu'ukohala
Heiau is nearby (see Historic Sites below).

Chocolate Factory

195. **Kailua Candy Company**—74-5552C Kaiwi St., Kailua-Kona.
The Kailua Candy Company creates world-class
chocolates using Kona products such as Kona coffee,
macadamia nuts, guavas, and others. They offer tasting
tours and free transportation from Kona and Keauhou
hotels. Open 9:00am to 5:00pm Monday through Friday,
and 9:00am to noon on Saturday. Call 329-2522 or
1-800-MAC-CHOC.

Entertainment

196. **Kimo's Restaurant**—*at* Uncle Billy's Kona Bay Hotel, *across from* Kona Inn Shopping Village, Kailua-Kona. Kimo's has a hula show every evening at 6:30pm and 7:30pm. Call 329-1393 for more information.

197. **Fashion Show**—*Fisherman's Landing,* Kona Inn Shopping Village, 75-5744 Alii Drive, Kailua-Kona. Every Friday from 12:30pm to 1:30pm, mall merchants sponsor an elaborate fashion show featuring everything from casual sportswear to elegant evening wear. Call 326-2555 for more information.

198. **Akaka Falls Flea Market**—*next to* Ishigo General Store *in* Honomu. Flea markets are always a fun way to see local trash and treasures, and this one advertises itself as the "biggest little flea market in the world." It's worth a stop on the way to Akaka Falls. Open daily from 9:00am to 5:00pm.

Gardens

199. **Akatsuka Orchid Gardens**—*Highway 11 at the 22-mile marker from Hilo on the way to Volcano.* This farm grows orchids of all varieties, colors, and sizes and displays them in their natural settings. You can stroll through the covered gardens and receive a free orchid just for visiting. Open daily 8:30am to 5:00pm. Phone: 967-7660.

200. **Glover Orchids**—*off* Highway 19 *at* Kalaoa junction, 73-4392 Pukiawe St., Kailua-Kona. This orchid farm also welcomes visitors with a free orchid. Phone: 326-2077.

201. **Hata Farm**—*in* Kurtistown *on* Highway 11 *between* Hilo *and* Volcano. Hata's, an anthurium farm, is open to the public from 8:00am to 4:00pm. Phone: 966-9240.

Liliuokalani Gardens, one of the largest formal oriental gardens outside Japan.

202. **Hawaiian Flower Gardens Nursery**—*Highway 11, Mountain View at 14-mile marker.* Another anthurium garden which features fascinating hybrids. Open Monday through Friday from 8:30am to 4:30pm, and Saturday from 9:00am to 4:00pm. Phone: 968-6055.

203. **Hilo Tropical Gardens**—*1477 Kalanianaole Ave., Hilo.* This two-acre garden features colorful tropical flowers, shrubs, trees, and numerous species of orchids in a natural setting. It's a great spot for photo buffs to capture a variety of exotic orchids. They also offer a free hula show every Saturday at 10:00am. Phone: 935-4957.

204. **Liliuokalani Gardens**—*Banyan Drive, Hilo.* This elaborate, 30-acre park—one of the largest formal oriental gardens outside Japan—is filled with a variety of ornamental stone structures from Japan. It was named after Hawaii's last reigning monarch. Open daily from 6:00am to 11:00pm. Phone: 961-8311.

205. **Manuka State Park**—*Highway 11, between Ho'okena and Na'alehu.* This botanical garden has picnic areas and signs indicating the various flora grown on the Big Island. Always open. Phone: 961-7200.

206. **Wakefield Botanical Gardens**—*off Highway 11 at Honaunau.* Wakefield's has an interesting self-guided tour through their tropical flowers and plants. The garden is open from 8:00am to sunset. Phone: 328-9930.

Garment Factory

207. **Hilo Hattie Fashion Center**—*75-5597A Palani Road in Kailua-Kona, and 933 Kanoelehua St. in Hilo.* Hilo Hattie offers daily tours of their garment factory, where you can see colorful island fabrics made into muumuus, aloha shirts, and other resort wear. They also offer a lei and complimentary refreshments, as well as transportation in Hilo or Kona. Call 329-7200 for more information.

Visitors Bureau

208. **Hawaii Visitors Bureau**—*180 Kinoole in Hilo, and the Kona Plaza in Kailua-Kona.* The HVB has plenty of free sightseeing information and brochures for visitors. Also, when driving around, look for their red-and-yellow Hawaiian warrior markers along the roadside—they alert you to historic and cultural attractions. Call 961-5797 (Hilo) or 329-7787 (Kona).

Hirano Store

209. **Hirano's**—*Highway 11, Volcano Road at 20 mile marker.* They claim to have the best view of Kilauea's pu'u o'o vent. They

also offer a free anthurium to all visitors. Open daily. Call 968-6522.

Historic Sites

210. **Ahu'ena Heiau & Kamakahonu National Historic Site—** *adjacent to the* Hotel King Kamehameha, Kailua-Kona. This restored site was the headquarters of Kamehameha the Great, who united the Islands into one kingdom. He died at this spot in 1819. The Ahu'ena Heiau, a former temple, served as the seat of the Hawaiian government during the last seven years of Kamehameha's reign. The Hotel King Kamehameha offers guided tours of the grounds, including their displays of Hawaiian artifacts and plants. Tours at 1:30pm daily. Phone: 329-2911.

211. **Hulihee Palace—** Alii Drive, *next to the seawall*, Kailua-Kona. Built in 1838 of coral and lava, this former summer retreat of many Hawaiian monarchs was used by royalty until 1916. It was restored by the Daughters of Hawaii and is now operated as a museum. There is an admission fee to visit the inside (open 9:00am to 4:00pm daily), but you can tour the grounds for free. Phone: 329-1877.

212. **Kamehameha Statue—***off* Highway 270 *in* Kapa'au. This is the original Kamehameha Statue which was cast in Florence, Italy in 1880 and was lost at sea on its journey to Honolulu. A replica was made, which now stands in front of the Judiciary Building on Oahu. The original was later recovered and installed in Kapa'au near Kamehameha's birthplace.

213. **Kealakekua Bay—***off* Highway 11 *near* Napoopoo. This beautiful bay is the site where the famous British explorer Captain Cook landed and met his death in 1779. There is a Captain Cook Monument across the bay, and a large lava structure, the Hikiau Heiau, where Hawaiians once

The original statue of Kamehameha, in front of the Kapaau Courthouse.
(Photo courtesy County of Hawaii)

worshipped Captain Cook as the god Lono. The bay is a marine preserve and offers great snorkeling, swimming, and camping.

214. **Keauhou Bay**—*at the end of Alii Drive at Keauhou.* On the grounds of the Keauhou Beach Hotel, there are ancient petroglyphs and *heiaus.*

215. **Lapakahi State Historical Park**—*Highway 270 near Mahukona Beach Park.* Lapakahi was an important and busy harbor in the days of the Hawaiian monarchy, and the historical park was once an ancient seaside village. It's

open Monday through Saturday from 8:00am to 4:00pm and has self-guided tours. Phone: 889-5566.

216. **Mokuaikaua Church**—*Alii Drive, Kailua-Kona, across from the Hulihee Palace.* Built in 1836, this church was the first Christian church in the islands. Services are still held each Sunday in Hawaiian and English. Visitors are welcome.

217. **Mo'okini Heiau**—*off Highway 270 on a side road near the Upolu Airport.* This ancient site was once the location of a sacrificial temple built with stones passed hand to hand from the coast—nine miles away! It's a bit of an adventure to get to there, but it's worth the effort.

218. **Puako Petroglyphs**—*end of Puako Beach Road, Puako.* The acres and acres of mysterious carvings at Puako are thought to be some of the oldest petroglyphs in Hawaii. Historians and scientists still speculate about the significance of these rock carvings found throughout the islands.

219. **Puukohola Heiau**—*near Kawaihae harbor and Spencer Beach Park.* This national historic site was originally built around 1550 and was rebuilt by Kamehameha I in 1791. He invited his last remaining rival on the Big Island there—and killed him.

220. **St. Benedict's "Painted Church"** —*off Highway near Ho-* *naunau.* One of the Big Island's quaint old churches, St. Benedict's was painted around the turn of the century by its priest, who wanted to give it the look of a European cathedral.

Tropical Paintings

221. **St. Peter's "Little Blue Church"** —*adjacent to Kahalu'u Beach near the Keauhou Beach Hotel.* This tiny blue-and-white chapel was built in 1880 on the foundation of an ancient Hawaiian temple.

222. **Star of the Sea Painted Church**—*Kalapana*. The 1977 lava flow stopped just 400 yards short of destroying this charming old church, built in 1931 and decorated with religious frescoes along the walls and ceiling.

Kailua Wharf

223. **Kailua Wharf**—*Alii Drive, Kailua-Kona*. At this wharf you can see Kona's sportfishing fleet weigh-in their big catches daily between 4:00pm and 5:00pm.

Macadamia Nuts

224. **Hawaiian Holiday Macadamia Nut Factory**—*Route 19 in Honokaa, and Kona Inn Shopping Village, Alii Drive, Kailua-Kona*. Visitors can observe how macadamia nuts are processed and made into a variety of tasty products and also get free samples. Open daily 9:00am to 6:00pm. Phone: 775-7255.

225. **Mauna Loa Macadamia Nut Factory**—*5 miles south of Hilo off Route 11*. There are several macadamia nut factories around the island, but this is probably the biggest. The entrance road is a three-mile drive through the largest macadamia nut orchard in the world. Their visitor center contains a video program describing the whole process the nuts go through, from planting to harvesting to processing. You can also enjoy free samples, take a walk on their nature trail, or watch the processing plant in action. Open daily from 9:00am to 5:00pm. Phone: 966-8612.

226. **Mrs. Field's Macadamia Nut Factory**—*Halekii St., off Highway 11 in Kealakekua*. This macadamia nut factory has the added attraction of being run by the Mrs. Fields Cookie Company. So, after viewing the processing plant, visitors are treated to samples of Mrs. Fields cookies.

Guided tours are conducted every half hour from 8:30am to 5:30pm daily. Phone: 322-9515.

Museums

227. **Mauna Kea Royal Kona Coffee Mill and Museum**—*above Kealakekua Bay, near Captain Cook.* For 150 years, the Kona District on the Big Island has been the source of one of the world's great coffees, which is also the only coffee grown commercially in the U.S. At the Royal Kona Coffee Mill and Museum, visitors can sample Kona coffee, browse through a photo gallery, and learn about coffee growing and processing. Open daily from 8:00am to 4:30pm. Phone 328-2511.

228. **Pacific Museum Studios and Gallery**—*Waiohino off Highway 11.* Tour the studios, sculpture garden, and historic displays and see artisans at work at the Pacific Museum. Open from 9:00am to 5:00pm, but call first. Phone: 929-9101.

229. **Punaluu Village Museum**—*adjoining the Punaluu Black Sands Restaurant, Punaluu.* This small but interesting museum is operated by C. Brewer & Co., one of Hawaii's giant sugar firms, and contains old photos of C. Brewer's history. There is also a video program about the volcano's activity and a mural by artist Herb Kane. Open daily from 10:30am to 3:00pm. Phone: 928-8528.

Star Gazing

230. **Mauna Kea Observatory**—*atop Mauna Kea.* Every Saturday evening, the observatory at the 13,796-foot peak of Mauna Kea is open for visitors to enjoy some of the best star gazing in the world. A caravan leaves the Hale Pohaku

nite time

Visitors Center at the 9,000-foot level at 6:30pm and arrives at the summit at 9:30pm. Call 935-3371 for reservations.

Parks

231. **Lava Tree Park**—*Kapoho Point, off Route* 132. A ten-minute stroll through a unique park follows strange lava formations created by a lava flow in 1790. Beyond the park, toward the ocean at Kapoho, everything was destroyed in a 1960 eruption, except the lighthouse and a house next to an ancient Hawaiian *heiau*.

232. **Wailoa State Park**—*off Kamehameha Ave. in Hilo*. This area was part of the business district before it was destroyed during the last tidal wave to hit Hilo in 1960. The park contains the Wailoa Visitor Center, which features art and cultural exhibits. Closed Sundays. Phone: 961-7360.

Publications

233. Free travel literature is available around the island at shopping centers, car rental agencies, hotels, and other distribution points. Look for *Hawaii Island Guide*, *This Week*, *Big Island Drive Guide*, and others. They all contain maps, calendars of events, discount coupons, as well as travel tips.

Scenic Attractions

234. **Akaka Falls**—*end of Highway* 220 *above Honomu*. This state park contains one of Hawaii's most spectacular waterfalls. There's a short walk through a tropical forest of ginger, bamboo, orchids, and other plants, then a stop at Hapuna

Falls, a smaller (100-foot) waterfall. Further on is Akaka Falls, the 420-foot spectacle.

235. **Pololu Valley Lookout**—*end of* Highway 270, *past* Kapaau. This 360-degree view of mountains, valley, and sea overlooks the site where stones were passed by hand up the coast for nine miles to build the Mo'okini *heiau.*

236. **Rainbow Falls**—*Wailuku* River State Park, *off* Waianuenue Ave., Hilo. The morning is the best time to view this impressive waterfall, because the early sunshine produces rainbows in the mist at the bottom of the falls. The park is open from 8:00am to 7:00pm.

237. **South Point**—11 *rough miles off* Highway 11, *near* Wai'ohinu. South Point is the southernmost point in the United States. It's believed that Polynesians first landed there around 150 A.D. There are still remains of Kalalea Heiau at the end of the road, plus a a green sand beach.

238. **Waipio Valley Lookout**—*end of* Highway 240. This dramatic site, one of Hawaii's best panoramic views, overlooks a verdant 2,000-foot gorge. The valley was once home to over 50,000 Hawaiians.

Tennis

239. **Kailua Playground** in Kailua-Kona, **Lincoln Park** in Hilo (Kinoole and Ponahawai Streets), and **Waimea Park** in Waimea all have free tennis courts.

TV Tour

240. Cable TV **Channel 6** offers a television tour of the Big Island every day from 6:00am to 6:00pm and 9:30pm to

6:00am, featuring volcanic eruptions, thundering waterfalls, big game fishing, and other spots you may not have time to visit. Call 322-3672 for more information.

Zoo

✱✱✱ (241) **Panaewa Rainforest Zoo**—*Mamakai St. off Highway 11 near Hilo.* The only rainforest zoo in the U.S., Panaewa receives over 125 inches of rain a year. The zoo displays animals from rainforests around the world. There are also picnic areas. Open daily 9:00am to 4:00pm. Phone: 959-9233.

Island of Hawaii Annual Events

April
242. **Merrie Monarch Festival**—*Hilo.* This is one of the biggest happenings on the Big Island each year. Ancient and modern hula are performed by several *halau* (schools) during this week-long festival. There is also a parade and other entertainment held in Hilo. Though there is a charge for some of the performances, many events are free. For exact dates and locations, call 935-9168.

May
243. **Quarterhorse Show**—*Waikoloa Stables* The island's best riders compete with their horses in this annual show. Call 885-4515 for more information.

June
244. **King Kamehameha Day Celebration**—*Kailua-Kona and Hilo.* Kamehameha Day, June 11, is a state holiday, and celebrations are held throughout the islands. There is a parade in Kailua-Kona and entertainment, craft exhibits,

and other festivities in Hilo. Call 935-9338 or 329-5338 for exact dates, locations, and times.

July

245. **Parker Ranch Rodeo**—*Paniolo Park in Waimea*. On the 4th of July weekend, the employees of Parker Ranch compete in the rodeo events of calf-roping, double mugging, and bull-riding. Call 885-7655 for date and time.

August

246. **Hawaiian International Billfish Tournament**—*Kailua-Kona*. There's always lots of activity on the Kailua-Kona pier during the annual Billfish Tournament. Bleachers are erected on the pier for spectators, and there's a parade and opening ceremonies. Call 922-9708 on Oahu.

September

247. **Aloha Week Festival**—*island-wide*. Aloha Week is filled with athletic events, luaus, canoe races, a parade, street parties, and other activities. Call 944-8857 on Oahu.

October

248. **Bud Light Ironman Triathlon World Championship**—*Kailua-Kona*. This grueling event includes a 2.4-mile ocean swim, followed by a 112-mile bicycle race and a 26.2-mile marathon run. The course begins and ends at the Kailua Pier. Athletes from around the world travel to the Big Island for this annual event, which supposedly began after a barroom bet over who was the better athlete—a swimmer, biker, or runner. First held in 1978, it now has over 15,000 applicants. Call 322-4766.

November

249. **Kona Coffee Festival**—*Kailua-Kona*. The Kona Coffee Council sponsors this annual event, which features a parade, coffee recipe contests, and other activities. Call 322-6500.

Island
of
Kauai

Kauai, the oldest and fourth largest of Hawaii's main islands, is a verdant gem nicknamed the "Garden Island." It has the distinction of having the wettest spot on earth, Mount Waialeale, which receives over 450 inches of rain annually.

Sugar cane was first introduced to Hawaii at Lihue, one of the oldest plantation towns in the Islands. Kauai is also the site of the first landing of the Polynesians (about 1,000 years ago) and of the British explorer Captain Cook in 1778.

One of the most impressive sights in all of Hawaii is surely Kauai's Waimea Canyon, a rugged gorge that cuts 2,857 feet into the Kokee Plateau. Often called "the Grand Canyon of the Pacific," the canyon borders Kokee State Park, an expansive wilderness area with over 45 miles of hiking trails and the Kokee Natural History Museum.

Legends abound on Kauai about the *menehune,* a race of little people who worked only at night and who supposedly built the mysterious fish ponds near Nawiliwili Harbor.

A gorgeous area along Kauai's northern side is the Na Pali coast, accessible only by boat or on foot. The highway ends at Haena, where an 11-mile trail leads to Kalalau Valley, a pristine and remote area filled with fruit trees, ancient taro patches, streams, and waterfalls.

Kauai's beauty is so spectacular that it is often selected for television and film settings. More than any other Hawaiian island, Kauai still maintains the image of paradise.

Art

250. **Artisans Guild of Kauai**—*above the Ching Young Store in Hanalei*. This co-op displays the works of over 30 island artists, including stained glass, batik, photography, shellcraft, and a variety of paintings and graphics. Open daily 10:00am to 6:00pm. Phone: 826-6441.

251. **Kauai Crafts in Progress**—*1384 Kuhio Highway in Kapaa*. This store features Kauai-made arts and crafts, and you can watch the artisans painting tiles and making dolls, jewelry, and Christmas tree ornaments. Open Monday through Friday 9:00am to 5:00pm. Phone: 822-7558.

252. **Stones Gallery**—*at Kilohana on Kaumualii Highway*. Featuring arts and crafts of Hawaii and the South Pacific, Stones Gallery is located on the grounds of the Kilohana Plantation. Open Monday through Saturday 10:00am to 7:30pm, and Sunday 10:00am to 5:00pm. Phone: 245-6684.

Beaches

253. **Anini Beach**—*near Kilauea*. This well-protected beach, practically deserted during the week, offers excellent snorkeling in the summer.

254. **Lumahai Beach**—*North Shore between Hanalei and Haena*. This beautiful beach became famous after part of the movie *South Pacific* was filmed there. Swimming is safe in the summer only.

255. **Poipu Beach Park**—*Poipu Road to Hoowili Road (which ends at Hoone Road)*. Poipu is one of the best spots on the island to picnic, swim, and snorkel.

Kauai

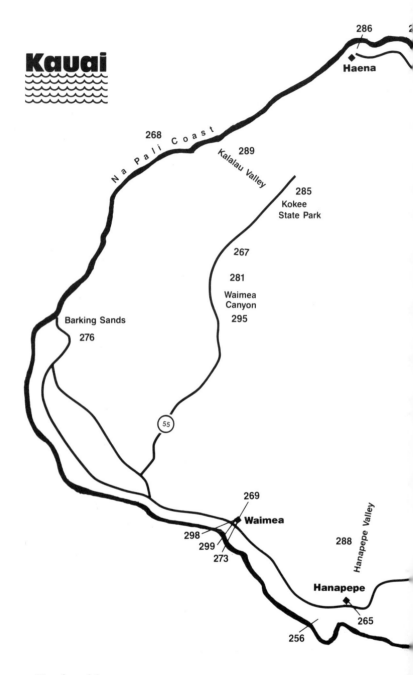

286

Haena

268 Na Pali Coast

289
Kalalau Valley

285
Kokee
State Park

267

281

Waimea
Canyon
295

Barking Sands
276

55

269
Waimea

298
299
273

288

Hanapepe Valley

Hanapepe

265

256

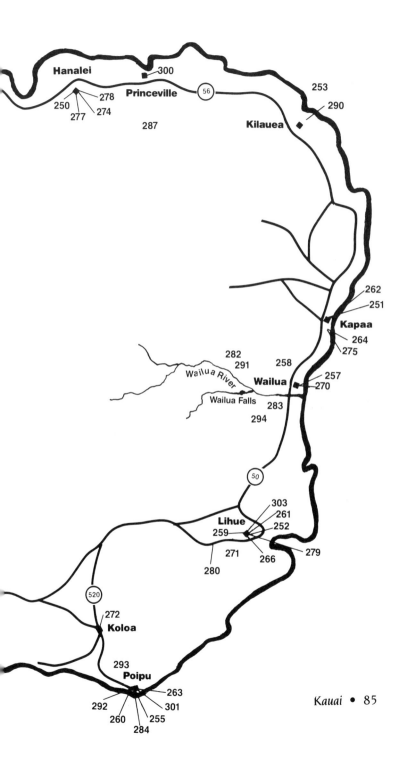

Hanalei

300

Princeville

56

253

290

250 278
277 274

287

Kilauea

262
251

Kapaa

264
275

282
291

258

Wailua River

Wailua

257
270

Wailua Falls

283
294

50

303
261
Lihue 252
259

271 266 279

280

520

272

Koloa

293

Poipu 263
301
292 255
260
284

256. **Salt Pond Beach Park**—*outside Hanapepe off Highway* 543. This swimming beach was named for the nearby ponds which were the source of salt for ancient Hawaiians. During the summer months you can still see local families collect the salt crystals that have been dried in wells and aging ponds.

Demonstrations

257. **Jewelry-making**—*Goldsmith's Gallery, Kinipopo Shopping Village, Wailua.* Learn how fine jewelry is made by watching craftsmen at work. Open Monday through Friday 9:30am to 7:00pm, and Saturday 9:30am to 6:00pm. Phone: 822-4653.

258. **Lei- and quilt-making**—*The Market Place at Coconut Plantation in Kapaa.* This center has daily demonstrations and entertainment and offers free shuttle service from many hotels and the harbor. Open Monday through Saturday 9:00am to 9:00pm, and Sundays 9:00am to 5:00pm.

Entertainment

259. **Movies at the Libraries**—*Lihue Library, 4344 Hardy St., Lihue.* Every Tuesday at 7:00pm, the Lihue library shows free movies. Call 245-3617 for the title of the movie of the week. And Wednesday at 7:00pm, the Koloa Library on Poipu Road shows movies. Call 742-1635.

260. **"Twilight Polynesian Revue"** —*Kiahuna Shopping Village at Poipu Beach.* Leilani's Keiki Hula Halau performs Monday and Thursday at 5:30pm and Sunday at 4:30pm.

261. **Square Dancing**—*by Paradise Promenaders, Lihue Neighborhood Center, off Kuhio Highway.* The Paradise Promenaders dance every Friday from 7:30pm to 9:30pm. If

you'd like to join them, it will cost $1.00, but you can watch for free. Call 822-4836 for more information.

262. **Polynesian Show**—*The Market Place at Coconut Plantation in Kapaa*. Costumed dancers perform Polynesian hula to live music every Thursday, Friday, and Saturday at 4:00pm.

263. **Komo Mai Bridge Club**—*Poipu Kai Restaurant in the Poipu Kai, 1941 Poipu Road in Koloa*. The club meets every Tuesday at 7:00pm, and the public is invited.

Gardens

264. **Kinipopo Botanical Garden**—*Kinipopo Shopping Village, south of Kapaa*. This center contains a lovely collection of tropical trees and plants. A descriptive guide can be obtained free at most shops in the complex.

265. **Shimonishi Orchids**—*3567 Hanapepe Road in Hanapepe*. Shimonishi has Kauai's most extensive selection of orchids. The Shimonishi family has spent the last 40 years raising some of the world's most beautiful orchids, including several award-winning hybrids. Open Monday through Saturday 8:00am to 4:00pm. Phone: 335-5562.

Garment Factory

266. **Hilo Hattie's Fashion Center**—*3252 Kuhio Highway, near the airport*. Hilo Hattie's will pick up visitors from hotels in the Coconut Plantation and Lihue areas and provide complimentary refreshments, a lei, and a tour of their factory, where you can watch colorful island fabrics made into resort wear. Call 245-3404.

Hiking

(267.) **Kokee State Park**—*near Waimea Canyon*. This 4,345-acre park has over 45 miles of hiking trails. Detailed information and maps are available at the park headquarters. Hikers should register at the headquarters before going out and when they return. There are several short, easy trails within the park—good for families and others who are not into strenuous walking. Hiking enthusiasts can write the Dept. of Land and Natural Resources (PO Box 1671, Lihue, Kauai, HI 96766) for lists and maps of trails on Kauai.

(268) **Na Pali Coast**—*end of Kuhio Highway in Haena*. This coastline, Kauai's most famous wilderness area, offers some of the most stunning scenery in Hawaii. The whole trail is 11 miles long and is recommended only for hardy hikers, but others can enjoy the first two to four miles of the trail, with a secluded beach, beautiful waterfalls, and pools along the way. Begin at Kee Beach at the end of Kuhio Highway, and sign the log book at the trailhead. It's two miles to Hanakapiai Beach, and another two miles to the waterfall at the top of the valley.

Beginning of 11 mile Hike

Historic Sites

269. **Captain Cook Monument**—*Waimea*. This historic town is where Captain James Cook first landed in the Sandwich Islands in 1778. In addition to the statue which pays tribute to the famous explorer, Waimea has a number of buildings on the National Register of Historic Places.

270. **Holo Holo Ku Heiau**—*Kuamoo Road, Wailua*. This is perhaps the oldest *heiau* on Kauai and is where human sacrifices were made. A few yards away is the Pohaku Ho'o Hanau, a collection of sacred stones where royal women gave birth.

The Menehune Fishpond, supposedly built by a race of "little people."

271. **Menehune Fishpond**—*Niumalu Road off Route 51, near Nawiliwili. (At times there is an HVB warrior marker at the lookout point for this attraction, but it seems to disappear from time to time, so look for the green guardrail.)* One of Kauai's most famous legends concerns this fishpond. It's said to have been built by the *menehune*, a race of tiny Polynesian people who were supposedly Kauai's first residents. The legend says that the *menehune* consented to build the pond overnight for a princess and her brother, on the condition that no one watch them as they worked. But the two couldn't resist the temptation to have a peek. They were discovered watching, and the *menehune* turned them into stone pillars, which still stand on the side of the mountain. Whatever its origin, the fishpond is a beautiful spot.

272. **Old Koloa Town**—*Highway 520.* This area was originally a plantation town established in 1835, when three New Englanders leased land from King Kamehameha III. The town has been restored and now houses shops,

restaurants, and other services. In the center of the court-yard, a little museum area displays interesting historic photos. Open 9:00am to 9:00pm daily.

273. **Russian Fort (Fort Elizabeth)**—*east end of Waimea*. This fort was constructed in the early 1800's under an alliance between the Russian-American Company and Kauai's King Kaumualii. Not much remains of the fort, but the State of Hawaii has prepared an informative brochure and map of the area which describes it as it was in the 1800s. The brochures are in a shed in front of the fort.

274. **Waioli Mission House**—*Hanalei*. This restored missionary home belonged to Rev. William P. Alexander, an American missionary who arrived on Kauai in 1834. The home was restored in 1921 by the Wilcox family and is listed on the National Register of Historic Places. Half-hour guided tours through the home are offered on Tuesday, Thursday, and Saturday from 9:00am to 3:00pm. Phone: 245-3202.

Information Center

275. **Kauai Visitor Center**—*The Market Place at Coconut Plantation in Waipouli, and 3122 Kuhio Highway in Lihue*. These folks assist visitors in finding the best activities at reasonable prices. They will make reservations for you and provide information about sights and activities, and their service is free. Phone: 245-3882.

Missile Range

276. **Pacific Missile Range**—*end of Highway 50 on Barking Sands Beach*. The Range offers tours on the first and third Wednesday of each month by reservation. The tour lasts

about 1½ hours and includes a film, visits to the target ranges, and an opportunity to board the helicopters. Call 335-4243 for reservations.

Museums

277. **Hanalei Museum**—*Highway 56 in Hanalei.* This small museum houses many pictures of Hanalei during the rice-growing period, as well as photographs of the destruction caused by the *tsunamis* of 1946 and 1957. The building dates back to the 1860s and also contains Hawaiian artifacts and other memorabilia. Open 10:00am to 4:00pm Monday through Friday, and 10:00am to 3:00pm on Saturdays. Phone: 826-6783.

278. **Hawaiian Cultural Center**—*Ching Young Village in Hanalei.* A fascinating collection of artifacts, antiques, and photographs are scattered throughout the displays of new merchandise. Open daily from 10:00am to 6:00pm.

279. **Kauai Museum**—*4428 Rice St., Lihue.* There is normally an admission charge to this museum, Kauai's largest; however, the first Saturday of each month is free. The museum houses Hawaiian geological and cultural exhibits, as well as changing art exhibits. Open Monday through Friday 9:30am to 4:30pm, and Saturday from 9:00am to 1:00pm. Phone: 245-6931.

280. **Kilohana**—*two miles outside Lihue on Highway 50.* This restored 1930 plantation estate of Gaylord Park Wilcox sits on 35 acres of tropical gardens. The home contains many museum-quality art works and memorabilia. You can tour the home and grounds, which contain "Kilohana Camp," a century-old plantation village. Open from 9:00am to 7:00pm daily. Phone: 245-5608.

281. **Kokee Natural History Museum**—*Kokee State Park*. This museum houses exhibits of Kauai's bird and plant life, as well as geographic maps of the island, including the hiking trails. Open from 10:00am to 4:00pm daily. Phone: 335-9975.

Parks

282. **Keahua Arboretum**—*at the end of* 580. Here you can wander the trails among the eucalyptus trees and other exotic flora, or have a picnic and lie in the sun in a wonderfully tranquil setting.

283. **Lydgate State Park**—*off* Highway 56 *near the mouth of the Wailua River*. The remains of an ancient temple of refuge still stand in this park. In ancient times, if someone had broken a *kapu* (taboo) but could make it to this sacred spot, no one could harm him.

284. **Prince Kuhio Park**—*Lawai Road near Poipu*. A monument dedicated to the birthplace of Prince Kuhio stands in the middle of this small park across the street from the ocean. It's a nice spot for a sunset picnic.

285. **Kokee State Park**—*follow* Highway 550 *to the park headquarters and Kokee Lodge*. With over 4,000 acres of wilderness, including 45 miles of hiking trails ranging from family nature walks to rugged treks, Kokee has something for everyone. The Kokee Natural History Museum, located next to the Kokee Lodge, has maps of the trails.

Scenic Attractions

286. **Caves**—*Maniniholo, Waikanaloa and Waikapalea, in Haena*. These small caves are actually lava tubes with vaulted ceilings. They have been visitor attractions since the 1800's,

and local legends attribute their origins to the *menehune* and to Madame Pele.

287. **Hanalei Valley Lookout**—*just past* Princeville Shopping Center, Highway 56. One of the most photographed spots on Kauai, the broad panorama of the taro patches and majestic mountains in the background evoke the memory of Hawaii of long ago. The bridge was built in 1912 and is now on the National Register of Historic Places.

288. **Hanapepe Canyon Lookout**—Highway 50. The last battle fought on Kauai took place directly opposite this lookout which scans the Hanapepe Valley, once the site of a Hawaiian settlement.

289. **Kalalau Lookout**—*near the end of* Highway 55. This verdant valley, where Hawaiian families once lived, is surrounded by rugged cliffs which plunge 4,000 feet to the ocean.

290. **Kilauea Point Lighthouse and Bird Refuge**—Kilauea Road. The Bird Refuge is the largest bird nesting area in Hawaii, and the lighthouse is situated dramatically above the ocean. There is an admission charge to tour the lighthouse, but you can admire it from the lookout for free.

291. **Opaekaa Falls**—*off* Highway 580. Although these falls are less dramatic than the Wailua Falls, they are still worth a visit, especially if you walk across the highway to the lookout for the magnificent view of the Wailua River.

292. **Spouting Horn**—Lawai Road near Poipu. Similar to the Blow Hole on Oahu, this shoreline lava tube shoots water as the waves roll in. This one also makes a strange moaning sound.

293. **Tree Tunnel**—Route 520 towards Poipu. On your way to Poipu, you'll pass through a tunnel of eucalyptus trees planted by Walter McBride at the turn of the century to beautify the sugar plantation landscape.

294. **Wailua Falls**—*at the end of* Highway 583. These twin water-falls were made famous by the "Fantasy Island" television program. Visit mid-morning to catch the rainbows above the pool.

295. **Waimea Canyon Lookout**—Highway 55. Sometimes called the "Grand Canyon of the Pacific," Waimea Canyon is one of Kauai's most dramatic natural spectacles. From the lookout, you can see most of the deep gorge which cuts into the Kokee Plateau. The hiking trails around the canyon are described at the Kokee Natural History Museum.

Tennis

296. There are nine public **tennis courts** on Kauai, located in Hanapepe, Kalawai, Kapaa, Kekaha, Koloa, Lihue, Wailua Homestead, Wailua Houselots and Waimea. To get the exact location and to reserve a court, go by the Parks and Permits Office, 4280A Rice St., in Lihue (open 7:45am to 4:00pm Monday–Friday, or call 245-1881).

Tours

297. **TV Tours**—Channel 3 in Princeville, Poipu, and Hanalei, and Channel 6 in Kapaa run an almost continuous program for visitors showing Kauai attractions, island history, and other tips. Call 332-8348 for details.

298. The **Waimea Public Library** on Kaumualii Highway sponsors an easy 1½-hour walk which they call "First in History." Among other attractions, you pass the site of Captain Cook's first Hawaii landing and Russian Fort Elizabeth. You can take a walk with a brochure provided by the library or go with a guide on Tuesday, Thursday, and Saturday at 10:00am and 2:00pm. Call 338-1226.

Kauai Annual Events

February

299. **Captain Cook Celebration**—*Waimea Town at Lucy Wright Park.* "Hawaiian Mardi Gras" features local entertainers, hula shows, food, canoe races, and more. It takes place at the mouth of the Waimea River, where Captain Cook first landed in the Islands.

March

300. **Women's Kemper Open**—*Princeville Golf Course.* This international golf tournament is the ultimate event in women's professional golf. Call 826-3580 for exact dates.

301. **Prince Kuhio Festival**—*Prince Kuhio Park in Poipu.* Prince Kuhio Day, a state holiday, is observed on Kauai with ceremonies and adornment of the Prince Kuhio Statue, which marks his birthplace. The ceremonies are followed by day-long Hawaiian entertainment, a parade, food, and craft booths.

May

302. **Lei Day**—May 1 is marked by colorful celebrations on all the islands. Each island has its own special lei: shells for Niihau, *mokihana* for Kauai, *ilima* for Oahu, *kaunaoa* for Lanai, *hinahina* for Kahoolawe, *kukui* flowers for Molokai, *lokelani* for Maui, and *lehua* for the Big Island. Lei Day provides an opportunity to observe Hawaii's finest lei makers in competition at the Kauai Museum.

June

303. **King Kamehameha Celebration**—*Lihue.* Kamehameha Day is a state holiday honoring Kamehameha the Great, Hawaii's first monarch. The celebrations feature a parade in Lihue, dances, and cultural programs around the island.

304. **O-bon Season**—Beginning in June and extending for ten weeks into August, a different Buddhist temple throughout the island hosts a *bon* dance every weekend. These festive Japanese folk dances are held annually to honor ancestral souls. Held outdoors on the grounds of the different temples, they are quite intriguing to watch.

October

305. **Aloha Week**—Throughout the island, there is a week-long celebration with special events, canoe races, street dances, a parade, and a variety of entertainment and stage shows.

Island
of
Molokai

$\mathcal{M}$olokai, a slipper-shaped island 37 miles long and 10 miles wide, has only one small town, Kaunakakai, which sports two hotels and a population of about 2,200. On the west end, the island's only major resort, Kaluakoi, sits on the best beach surrounded by an 18-hole golf course.

Molokai Ranch owns about half of the island, and over 6,000 head of cattle graze on its pastures. The Ranch also raises exotic animals such as giraffe, kudu, and antelope to sell to zoos and game preserves.

The highest sea cliffs in the world loom along the northern coast. They lead down to Kalaupapa Peninsula, a national park and home to a small community of Hansen's Disease (leprosy) patients. In 1866, Hawaii's Department of Health began exiling leprosy patients to the Kalaupapa Peninsula. Their existence was grim until the arrival of Father Damien, a Belgian Priest who dedicated his life to caring for the outcasts. Father Damien, who contracted the disease and died in 1889, is revered on Molokai. Once over 1,000 people lived at Kalaupapa; today about 100 remain.

At the east end of the island, the road ends at Halawa Valley, formerly home to hundreds of Hawaiians. Those who hike into the valley will be rewarded by the sight of a stunning 250-foot waterfall.

Molokai's only state park, Palaau, contains a campground, an arboretum, an overlook with a spectacular view of the cliffs, and an amusing phallic rock named *Ka Ule O Nanahoa*, which, according to legend, can cure a woman's infertility.

Kaunakakai is the site of the annual Molokai Mule Drag, which pits muleskinners against their stubborn beasts. Molokai is also the starting point for the annual Molokai-to-Oahu Outrigger Canoe Race in October.

Art

306. **Molokai Gallery**—*Kaunakakai*. This gallery features original Molokai glassware and creations in fabric, wood, clay, bark, and deerhorn by artists of Molokai. Open Monday through Friday 10:00am to 8:00pm, Saturday 10:00am to 6:00pm, and Sunday 10:00am to 3:00pm. Phone: 553-3392.

307. **Plantation Gallery**—*Maunaloa St., Maunaloa Town*. The Plantation Gallery exhibits paintings, scrimshaw, seed jewelry, batik, and other Island-made art works. Open 10:00am to 6:00pm.

Beaches

308. **Kepuhi**—*end of Kaluakoi Road*. The Kaluakoi Resort sits on Kepuhi, the best stretch of beach on Molokai. Papohaku Beach, just south of the resort, is also a beautiful white beach—good for picnicking but not for swimming.

Camping

309. **Palaau State Park**—*end of Highway 47*. This is the only state park on Molokai, and you'll need a permit to camp. The permit office is on Oahu at 1151 Punchbowl. Call 538-7455 for more information.

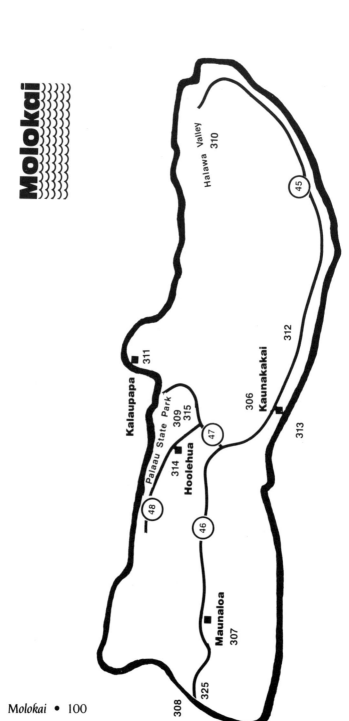

Molokai • 100

Hiking

310. **Halawa Valley**—*at the end of Highway 45 on the east side of the Island.* Near an abandoned church, a trail begins which winds two miles through a lovely green valley to a 250-foot waterfall and pool. This valley was heavily populated in ancient times, but today only a few families live there. The scene at the end of the trail is gorgeous and well worth the effort.

311. **Kalaupapa Trail**—*first left turn out of Palaau State Park.* For hardy hikers only, the Kalaupapa Trail is one of the most scenic spots in all of Hawaii. The trail zigzags down 1,600-foot cliffs to the Kalaupapa Peninsula, a National Park and home to about 100 people with Hansen's Disease. It's not possible to tour the settlement for free, but the trip down the trail is a worthwhile adventure. The trail is well-tended and not dangerous; it just takes a lot of energy to hike back up.

Historic Sites

312. **Our Lady of Sorrows Church**—*Highway 45.* Built by Father Damien in 1874, this church recently was restored. Father Damien went to Molokai in 1873 to work with the leprosy patients who had been banished to the Kalaupapa Peninsula. There's a whole row of quaint old churches along Highway 45.

Lessons

313. **Hawaiian Quilting**—*Hotel Molokai and Kaluakoi Resort.* Fiber artist Ginger LaVoie teaches quilting at the Hotel Molokai on Wednesday (phone 552-2555) and at the Kaluakoi Resort in the Gazebo on Friday (phone 553-5347) from 9:00am to noon.

A *well-maintained trail zigzags down these 1,600-foot cliffs to the Kalaupapa Peninsula.*

Macadamia Nut Farm

314. **Purdy's All Natural Macadamia Nut Farm**—*Lihipali Ave.,* *Hoolehua.* Purdy's offers a personalized tour through their 59-year old grove, giving information on macadamia nuts and Molokai's history, plus free samples of their products. Open daily from 9:00am to 1:00pm. Phone: 567-6601.

Scenic Attractions

315. **Palaau State Park**—*end of Highway* 47. This park has picnic tables and hiking trails and is forested with cypress, koa, and ironwood trees. One trail leads to Phallic Rock (which will leave you no doubt as to how it got its name), and another trail leads to the Kalaupapa Lookout, with a view of Kalaupapa Peninsula at the bottom of the 1,600-foot cliffs.

Of course, not everything in Hawaii can be free! Even so, the "best" does not mean that you have to break the bank. Whether you seek a secluded wilderness retreat or a swinging vacation resort, **Best Places to Stay in Hawaii** will help you find your ideal Hawaiian getaway. And the listing of best places to eat and play will direct you to Hawaii's most unique restaurants and sports facilities. So go ahead and get what you can for free, but when you have to spend a little, be sure to check **Best Places to Stay in Hawaii** first!

Please send check or money order made payable to The Harvard Common Press for $13.95 (Massachusetts residents add $.55 tax) to:

Sorry, no credit cards accepted.

Island
of
Lanai

*L*anai, the least-visited of Hawaii's main islands, reflects a lifestyle of another era. Though the 13,000 acres of pineapple fields give the island the look of a huge plantation, Lanai will reveal a special beauty and charm to the adventurous.

Most of the island's 140 square miles are owned by Castle and Cooke and are dedicated to pineapple growing. Most of Lanai's 2,300 residents work in the pineapple fields.

Lanai will appeal to travelers who enjoy exploring in a four-wheel drive vehicle. Oshiro's Service Station on Ninth Avenue gives visitors a map and advice on the best spots for snorkeling, swimming, hiking, or exploring archaeological sites.

Lanai City, the only town on the island, sits about 1,600 feet above sea level and has a very untropical atmosphere due to its cool climate and Norfolk pines. Lanaihale rises above the town, and the drive to the peak is spectacular. On a clear day you can see the Big Island, Oahu, Maui, and Molokai.

There are four treks around Lanai, including the Munro Trail (named after George Munro, a New Zealander who managed the Lanai Ranch in the early 1900's and who planted the Norfolk pines). The trail is over eight miles one way and goes from the drier part of the island up through the forest to much cooler temperatures.

The only recommended swimming beach is at Hulopo'e Bay, which lies at the end of Manele Road on the southern coast. A point of land juts out between Manele and Hulopo'e bays, where a small boat harbor and an attractive park are located. Hulopo'e has some of the clearest water and finest snorkeling in the Islands. Take some bread to feed the fish; they'll eat from your hand.

A visit to Kaunolu Village is an excursion into Lanai's fascinating past, to the days when Kamehameha the Great had a summer home there. There are still remains of the stone houses which once covered the area, and nearby is a cave that contains petroglyphs of sea birds. Kaunolu Village is thought to be the most complete archaeological site of its type in Hawaii.

A good fishing spot and beachcomber's delight is Shipwreck Beach, at the end of Keomuku Road. To the left is a trail to the beach, and to the right is Keomuku, the abandoned site of Maunalei Sugar Company and an old Hawaiian church.

Lanai has over 200 petroglyphs, some of which are the best-preserved in the islands. They are located throughout the island, but the Luahiwa petroglyphs are the most concentrated display.

Early Polynesians avoided Lanai because they believed it was inhabited by evil spirits. Today, the evil spirits have been displaced by a true feeling of *aloha* and a lifestyle of refreshing simplicity.

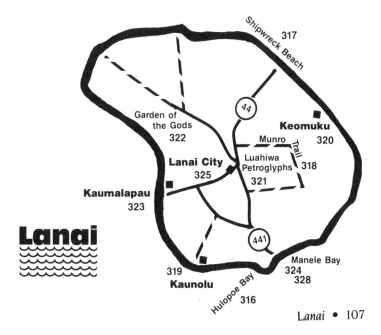

Hulopoe Bay, with some of the clearest water and best snorkeling in Hawaii.

Beaches

316. **Hulopoe Bay**—*at the end of Manele Road on the southern coast.* The only recommended swimming beach on Lanai, Hulopoe Bay has some of the clearest water and finest snorkeling in Hawaii. Take some bread, and the friendly fish will eat from your hand. Picnic tables and showers are available.

317. **Shipwreck Beach**—*end of Keomuku Road, turn left on a dirt road toward the beach.* This beach stretches for four miles and is a great spot for beachcombing. The remains of several ships that have hit the reefs have been washed ashore there. Though it's not a good place for swimming, the fishing is great.

Hiking

318. **Munro Trail**—*Highway 44 north, past the golf course and the first right turn onto a dirt road.* Named after a New Zealander who planted the Norfolk pines along the trail, the eight-mile Munro Trail goes from the drier part of the Island through the forest to Lanaihale, Lanai's highest point. The view from the top at 3,370 feet is lovely, and on a clear day you can see four Hawaiian islands in the distance.

Historic Sites

319. **Kaunolu Village**—*on the southwestern tip of the island.* You may need a four-wheel drive vehicle to visit this site, which contains some of the best-preserved ruins in the islands and was a favorite recreation area of Kamehameha the Great. At the end of a bumpy, three-mile trail, you can explore the ruins of the stone houses that once covered the area. There's also a once-inhabited cave containing petroglyphs of sea birds, as well as Kahekili's Jump. Kamehameha is said to have disciplined his soldiers by making them jump off the 60-foot cliff—and over a ledge that juts out 15 feet from the cliff below.

320. **Keomuku Village**—*at the end of Highway 44, turn right on the dirt road along the shoreline.* Keomuku is the abandoned site of a former sugar mill town owned by the Maunalei Sugar Company. There is also an old Hawaiian church, and further down the road is Naha, another old village site.

321. **Luahiwa Petroglyphs**—*on the road to Manele, take the dirt road off to the left and climb up the grassy slope. It's best to ask for directions.* Lanai has over 200 petroglyphs, some of which are the best-preserved in the islands. The Luahiwa petroglyphs are the most concentrated display on Lanai.

Lanai has some of the best-preserved petroglyphs in the Islands.
(Photo: Cindy Indermuehle)

Scenic Attractions

322. **Garden of the Gods**—*along* Awalua Road, *about seven miles from Lanai City.* At sunrise and sunset, this odd assortment of lava formations appears to change color and provides an interesting subject for photographers.

323. **Kaumalapau Harbor**—*six miles west on* Highway 440. If you time it right, you might see harvesting machines loading pineapples onto trucks, or hundreds of pickers gathering the fruit. It's also interesting to watch the barges in the harbor load and unload their cargo.

324. **Manele Bay**—*next to* Hulopoe Bay on the southern coastline. This small boat harbor is the landing site for most of the snorkeling cruise boats which come over from Maui.

325. **Swimming Pool**—*Lanai Community Center, Lanai Ave., Lanai City.* The pool at the Community Center is open to the public Tuesday-Friday from 12:30pm-6:30pm and Saturday from 10:00am-4:00pm. Call 565-6955.

Molokai and Lanai Annual Events

May

326. **Kanaka Ikaika (Molokai to Oahu Kayak Race), Kaluakoi Resort.** Men and women compete in this 32-mile, one-person kayak race from Molokai to Oahu across the Kaiwi Channel, one of the most treacherous channels in the world. A good place to watch the finish on Oahu is from the Koko Marina Shopping Center ocean promenade. Call 326-1011 for more information.

September

327. **Great Molokai Mule Drag, Kaunakakai.** Teams of "draggers" match wits and brawn against two dozen stubborn mules when they attempt to pull or coax them 300 yards. The team with the best time wins the "Grand Muleskinner Award." Following the contest there is a festival in the Kaunakakai Ball Park with Hawaiian entertainment. Call 567-6255 for more information.

September

328. **Lanai Swim, Manele Bay.** Swimmers compete in a six-mile rough-water swim from Manele Bay on Lanai to Lahaina Harbor on Maui.

More Great Travel Books from Mustang Publishing

Europe for Free by Brian Butler. If you think a trip to Europe is just one long exercise in cashing traveler's checks, then this is the book for you. The author describes *thousands* of activities, sights, and fun things to see and do—and nothing costs one single lira, franc, or pfennig. "A *valuable resource*"—U.P.I. **$9.95**

Europe: Where the Fun Is by Rollin Riggs & Bruce Jacobsen. No hotels, no museums, no historic sights. Just the wildest bars, the coolest nightclubs, the hottest beaches, the weirdest flea markets—just the fun stuff, in all the major cities of Europe. A terrific supplement to the major guidebooks. *Named one of the 25 best European travel guides by "Changing Times" magazine.* **$8.95**

The Student's Guide to the Best Summer Jobs in Alaska by Josh Groves. Thousands of young adults head for Alaska each summer, seeking jobs in the potentially lucrative fishing industry. Many return home with a lot of money; others come back hungry and broke. To succeed, you need information, and this is the most thorough book on the Alaska summer job scene available. "*Highly recommended*"—*The Tartan, Carnegie-Mellon Univ.* **$7.95**

Australia: Where the Fun Is by Lauren Goodyear & Thalassa Skinner. The "land down under" has become tops in travel, and these recent Yale graduates spent a year exploring both the tourist sites and the little-known back alleys all over Austalia and New Zealand. From the best pubs in Sydney to the cheapest motel in Darwin to the most spectacular treks around Ayers Rock, this book details all the fun stuff—on and off the beaten path. *Available November, 1988.* **$9.95**

———————

Mustang books should be available at your local bookstore. If not, order directly from us. Send a check or money order for the price of the book—plus $1.50 for postage *per book* —to Mustang Publishing, P. O. Box 9327, New Haven, CT 06533. Allow three weeks for delivery.

Add $3.50 per book for delivery in one week. Connecticut residents must add 7.5% sales tax. Foreign orders: U. S. funds only, please, and add $3.00 postage per book ($5.00 for Air Mail).